Ask the Masters!

Ask the Masters!

Scrapbook Solutions From the Memory Makers Masters

Edited by Darlene D'Agostino

Memory Makers Books
Cincinnati, Ohio
www.memorymakersmagazine.com

10 09 08 07 06   5 4 3 2 1

Distributed in Canada by Fraser Direct
100 Armstrong Avenue
Georgetown, ON, Canada L7G 5S4
Tel: (905) 877-4411

Distributed in the U.K. and Europe by David & Charles
Brunel House, Newton Abbot, Devon, TQ12 4PU, England
Tel: (+44) 1626 323200, Fax: (+44) 1626 323319
Email: postmaster@davidandcharles.co.uk

Distributed in Australia by Capricorn Link
P.O. Box 704, S. Windsor, NSW 2756 Australia
Tel: (02) 4577-3555

Library of Congress Cataloging-in-Publication Data
Ask the masters! : the editors at Memory Makers Books / Memory Makers Books.
    p. cm.
  Includes index.
  ISBN-13: 978-1-892127-88-4 (alk. paper)
  ISBN-10: 1-892127-88-1 (alk. paper)
  1. Photograph albums. 2. Photographs--Conservation and restoration. 3. Scrapbooks. I.
Memory Makers Books.
  TR501.A85 2006
  745.593--dc22
                            2006020277

Editor: Darlene D'Agostino
Designer: Marissa Bowers
Production Coordinator: Matt Wagner
Photographers: Christine Polomsky and Tim Grondin
Photo stylists: Jan Nickum and Leslie Brinkley

Turn the page for insight into the
Memory Makers Masters' tricks of the trade . . .

contents

Q & A WITH
the masters

What makes a master tick? What challenges her? Where does she find inspiration? Memory Makers sat down with all of our current and past masters to find out. Each is immensely passionate about this hobby, and each has her struggles. One thing almost all of them have in common? An affinity for Diet Coke!

Jessie Baldwin

Q: Who is/are your muse(s)?

A: I love listening to great music while I scrap, especially the Counting Crows. Any song with which I have an emotional attachment really boosts my creativity. I have a playlist on my iPod of songs that takes me through my teenage years, dating my husband, college, and other special memories.

Amber Baley

Q: What is one thing about scrapbooking that frustrates you?

A: I struggle with actually sitting down and doing a page. I put way too much into the preparation, and then I change it anyway. So many times I tell myself, "Just do it. Just sit down and work on the page." But I don't. I plan and waste so much time in the preparation.

Joanna Bolick

Q: Creative block—what do you do to overcome it?

A: Sometimes the best thing to do is STEP AWAY FROM THE SCRAPROOM. Take a shower, read a magazine, go outside—force yourself to concentrate on something else. If I need a jumpstart, I'll make a tag or card to get back into the creative process

Jennifer Bourgeault

Q: Do you have a ritual, habit or routine that you must practice before you begin scrapbooking?

A: My scrapbook room has to be clean before I can begin a project. Nor can I scrapbook without a Coke. I also just got a new radio for my scraproom and can no longer imagine scrapbooking without the tunes cranked up!

Jodi Amidei

Q: What's the best piece of constructive criticism you have ever received regarding your artwork?

A: I realized one day that I needed to be a better journaler. I kept explaining my scrapbook pages and photos to others—it made me see that if I still had more to say about the page it needed to be in the journaling, not in my mind.

Valerie Barton

Q: What is the first creative moment you remember?

A: Scrapbooking was my first creative moment. I never considered myself to be creative. I made my entire first book copying pages out of an idea book, but I wasn't happy with the result. I decided to try a page on my own. I loved the page! I realized I did have a creative core to my being and the more I explored it, the more it flourished.

Jenn Brookover

Q: What's the best piece of constructive criticism you have ever received regarding your artwork?

A: When I very first started, I had to cover every inch of the page in patterned paper, stickers or whatever I could find. A friend looked at my book and told me that I was "afraid of white space." She was right.

Sheila Doherty

Q: Do you have a ritual, habit or routine that you must practice before you begin scrapbooking?

A: I do like to work on layouts in at least two sittings. I like getting a layout started and then leaving it for a few hours (usually until the next day). Stewing over it really helps me put things together.

Katherine Brooks

Q: What is your creative ambition?

A: For a long time I think it was just to share my work with others, which I accomplished. Now it is to create just for myself and my family. I find that not sharing as much gives me more freedom in how I create. I do love to teach and travel, so that will always be my ambition.

Christine Brown

Q: What is one thing about scrapbooking that frustrates you?

A: I have commitment issues! I waste so much time shoving things around until it feels "perfect." It frustrates me that I am such a perfectionist. And if a design comes too quickly, I think there must be something wrong!

Susan Cyrus

Q: What is the first creative moment you remember?

A: One of my earliest memories is when I was a toddler I interrupted a dinner party my parents were hosting because I had found a pair of safety scissors, and I wanted my mother to teach me how to use them.

Kathy Fesmire

Q: Describe your creative process.

A: Sometimes a title comes to mind, sometimes a page theme or color scheme. As soon as I have the thought, I put it in my notebook. Once I have the sketch made, I list any specific products I know I want to use. Then I pull everything I am going to use to create the page. With my sketch beside me, I complete everything before I adhere anything to the page. Once it is all in place, I remove it all and begin to adhere the layers.

"I cannot keep my scrapbook supplies organized. If there is a path to my work table, I consider it a good day."

Jodi Amidei

> "I have to walk away from a project if I don't feel it. I can't force myself. If I do, the page looks totally wrong."
> **Julie Johnson**

Kelly Goree

Q: Creative block—what do you do to overcome it?

A: I love to visit the galleries of people whose work and ideas I admire. I also will peruse idea books and magazines. If all that fails, then I usually take a mini-hiatus to regroup and refocus.

Angie Head

Q: What is your creative ambition?

A: I am finally content with where I am creatively. I love being a freelance designer, and feel like I have come into my own with my own personal style. I know what I like and what I don't like. I can draw from current trends and yet not be dictated by them.

Jodi Heinen

Q: What is one thing about scrapbooking that frustrates you?

A: I am not good at follow through—I have so many half-finished theme albums. I have given up on finishing all the partially started albums. It used to bother me a lot, but now I am over it.

Diana Hudson

Q: What is one thing about scrapbooking that frustrates you?

A: I'd like to speed up the process. With all of the choices, I often find it difficult to make a decision. It's a lot easier when I make a few choices ahead of time.

Diana Graham

Q: Describe your creative process.

A: I must listen to music! Right now, I'm really into the Wicked soundtrack. I never look at my pages or projects as a chore. I scrap what I want, about whomever and always out of order. I just have never been very structured as an artist and cannot create by subscribing to a lot of rules. Whenever my page or project is complete it always goes up on display in my scrapbook room or on the shelves.

Nic Howard

Q: Describe your creative process.

A: My inspiration normally comes from conversation. For example, my daughter hung a teacup from my hubby's ear while we were all watching TV the other night. He left it there (we don't want to upset the two-year-old). He then tried to talk to me about something fairly serious. I said to him, "I can't take you seriously right now." Immediately that sparked a page idea on the things we have to do to keep the two-year-old happy.

Vanessa Hudson

Q: In regard to creativity, do you have a favorite quote or motto that inspires you?

A: There's no wrong way to be creative. There's no wrong way unless you're not being creative at all. You are the artist behind your project or layout, so the only one you have to please is yourself.

Suzy Plantamura

Q: What is the most recent scrapbooking-related lesson, technique or skill you have learned?

A: When I became a Master, I was so influenced by Danielle Thompson's work. She has this sense of freedom in her creations. My goal now is to have fun and just scrap in a free sort of way. I used to demand precision in my layouts—everything aligned and clean. Most of them had printed journaling. Now I hand write my journaling and, I doodle on my layouts. It is so FUN! I am an artist at heart, and this allows me to really explore my artistic side and creativity. The best tool that has helped me in this freestyle scrapping is the white gel pens Danielle told me about—Uni-ball Signo by Sanford.

Julie Johnson

Q: What's the best piece of constructive criticism you have ever received regarding your artwork?

A: You have to journal. If I look back at pages that I did three years ago, I still really love the ones with journaling. And the ones without? Well, all you can see are the "fads" of that period, like heavy inking or lots of metal.

Kelli Noto

Q: In regard to creativity, do you have a favorite quote or motto that inspires you?

A: My eleven-year-old son, Kevin, says, "Put your heart in your art." Sounds good to me!

Valerie Salmon

Q: Describe your creative process.

A: Having the latest and greatest products gets me in the mood to scrapbook! But the actual page always begins with the photos. They dictate the papers, embellishments and the whole layout design. I don't really have a set process. Some pages take an hour, some span days.

Heidi Schueller

Q: What is one thing about scrapbooking that frustrates you?

A: Timing. A lot of people probably think stay-at-home moms have tons of time. But we don't. I can't work on anything while the kids are around, and my studio is downstairs so I can't really watch them when they're outside from down there. I am usually scrapbooking very late, so I'm tired the next day. But I think everyone needs a passion, even if it isn't scrapbooking. It helps me retain who I am. I love being a mom and wife, but these roles don't define me. I am a person who needs this creative outlet to keep my sanity!

Torrey Scott

Q: Do you have a ritual, habit or routine that you must practice before you begin scrapbooking?

A: I take off my bra. Seriously. I truly believe my bra cuts off the creative flow of energy at my solar plexus, thus preventing it from reaching my hands. So OFF IT COMES! I also put on the most comfy clothes I can—either sweats and a T-shirt or jammies. I figure if I'm comfortable, my mind can focus on the art and not be otherwise preoccupied with my fidgeting body.

Jessica Sprague

Q: Do you have a ritual, habit or routine that you must practice before you begin scrapbooking?

A: Before I start a project, I say a quote from one of my favorite movies, Harold and Maude. Maude, who acts a little like Harold's creative muse in the movie, says to Harold, "Greet the dawn with a breath of fire." I love starting a project with energy and focus, and saying that helps me to be centered.

Shannon Taylor

Q: What is the first creative moment you remember?

A: It was at the beginning of my scrapbooking career. I was making those awful cutesy pages and decided to try "scraplifting" a wedding layout from the cover of an idea book. I added my own touch and realized there was a lot more to this hobby than I first thought.

Danielle Thompson

Q: What is your creative ambition?

A: I just want to create my art. As long as I continue to enjoy it, I will keep doing it, and I hope that in the process, I will inspire people.

Trudy Sigurdson

Q: In regard to creativity, do you have a favorite quote or motto that inspires you?

A: Scrapbookers need to scrapbook for themselves and their families, not to compete with their scrapbooking buddies or to be published in an online gallery or publication. It doesn't matter what other people think of your work. It only matters what you think and that you enjoy the process.

Denise Tucker

Q: What's the best piece of constructive criticism you have ever received regarding your artwork?

A: A friend of mine encouraged me to invest in a better camera so the quality of my photos would improve. It was worth every penny!

Samantha Walker

Q: What is the first creative moment you remember?

A: I remember scrounging around and pulling interesting items out of the trash to make projects. Empty toilet paper rolls were always a favorite—I loved to make soldiers out of them. I've been creating with trash and scraps ever since!

Lisa VanderVeen

Q: What is the most recent scrapbooking-related lesson, technique or skill you have learned?

A: I am actually learning to be a simpler scrapper. I have been technique-driven and very drawn to collage, but I have learned to appreciate the cleaner and colorful layouts. I sometimes have to make a conscious effort to walk away from a finished layout without adding more "stuff."

Susan Weinroth

Q: What's the best piece of constructive criticism you have ever received regarding your artwork?

A: "That page does not look like you; it doesn't look like your artwork." When my husband—who looks at every piece of artwork before I send it to be published—says that, I know that I've deviated from my own creative vision.

Sharon Whitehead

Q: Do you have a ritual, habit or routine that you must practice before you begin scrapbooking?

A: I don't have a ritual for scrapbooking, but the journaling process usually takes place while I am having a relaxing bath. There is no one to look over your shoulder, interrupt your train of thought or criticize what you write. It's just you and your thoughts, paper and pen.

Angelia Wigginton

Q: What is one thing about scrapbooking that frustrates you?

A: Most definitely a lack of space. I have a small desk against a wall in my bedroom, with no hope of anything larger. My supplies are terribly unorganized because there simply isn't enough space to accommodate even a quarter of it. It is a constant frustration. To overcome it, I'm adding shelves above my desk this week. I have nowhere to go but up, but it won't even begin to control the chaos.

Holle Wiktorek

Q: Describe your creative process.

A: Since the birth of my son, everything has changed. I used to focus on trendy products and techniques, but now my pages are about the story. I feel as if I am experiencing life for the first time again, through the eyes of my child, and I'm photographing it. These photos dictate the direction of the layout. The journaling now is the most important part because I want to tell my son about his life and how much he is loved.

"Inspiration can come from anywhere. By adopting this attitude, your eyes will open to wonders around you that you never noticed before. You'll be amazed."

Torrey Scott

Psst! In this chapter you will learn how to...

* emphasize your focal photo
* make group shots more fun
* take better travel photos
* be sneakier about taking candid photos
* use perspective to add interest to photos
* flatter a photo subject
* scrapbook retro photos
* create digital photo effects

FOCUS ON FABULOUS
photography

Photo tips and tricks to create dynamic images

Scrapbooking. It's all about the photos. These images are visual memories. So, why does it hafta be so hard to capture them? Sure, any monkey can take a photo, but an engaging image does not result from the mere press of a button. No, it's an act of creation.

The key to capturing stellar images is knowing the possibilities and limits of your camera, understanding light and having an eye for composition. While this chapter doesn't aim to be a crash course in photography, it is filled with tips to help you create better images.

Your camera is a tool, and just like any other tool, finesse in using it comes with time and practice. Read on to learn ways to make your focal photos pop right off their pages, how to manipulate perspective, get some ideas for scrapbooking retro photos and more.

What are some cool ways to make my focal photos pop? I mean, really pop!

The core, the heart, the marrow! That's what your focal photo is in regard to your layout. It requires and demands (demands, I say!) attention. The best way to make the photo pop is to first be sure that you have chosen the absolute best photo to showcase. The best photo is the one that evokes an emotional response. When picking a focal photo, spread the photos out and stare at them for a while. Which photo made you giggle or sigh? That's the focal photo, baby.

Alex, you are just the cutest thing. Here we were at Swan Lake Nature Sanctuary sitting and waiting for all of the other kids and parent drivers of your Grade 2 class to arrive and have a tour of the sanctuary to learn about bees. You are totally not bothered or embarrassed by having your Mum there...in fact you actually like it, so it does my heart good as I know that there will one day be a time when I am the last person you'll want hanging around you or driving for your class (especially since my camera is never far behind!). So for now, I'll savor every minute of it!

Alex

Trudy

SUPPLIES:
Patterned paper (Junkitz); letter stamps (Scraptivity); cardstock; brads; stamping ink; index tab (QuicKutz); date stamp (Just Rite Stampers); clear gloss medium; foam adhesive

Fun Photo Mat

When shopping the paper aisle at the scrapbook store, bold patterns are so tempting. But, once home, temptation can turn to frustration because the patterns tend to overwhelm photos. Trudy solves this problem by using such patterns in small doses. "The papers I used on this layout are very strong," Trudy says. "By cutting them into smaller blocks and layering them under and over a large photo, they add a funky design while still allowing the photo to take center stage."

Enlarge,
Crop Tight,
Add Color

The sheer size of this focal photo draws you in. But, what really makes it pop is the fact that it remains in color while the rest of the layout (photos, papers and accents) is black-and-white.

SUPPLIES:
Patterned paper (Basic Grey); chipboard letters (Heidi Swapp); metal monogram (source unknown); pens; stamping ink; cardstock

Kelly

Point to the Image

In regard to design, diagonal lines are an excellent way to create movement and direction. Here, Danielle uses them to full effect as they guide the eye directly to her focal photo. Several diagonal lines make up the background. They converge in the top right corner of the layout and radiate from there. The journaling strips that overlap and point directly to the photo are necessary to grab the reader's attention on this energetic page.

SUPPLIES:
Patterned paper (K & Co., Karen Foster Design, Paper Loft); buttons (Autumn Leaves); letter stickers (American Crafts); pen; dimensional paint; cardstock

Expert Advice!

More matting tricks to use for emphasizing a focal photo:

* Angle the mat behind the photo.

* Use a textured mat.

* Create a layered mat with papers in contrasting colors.

Danielle

17

Seriously, I'm sick of the groaning involved with taking group shots. How can I make it more fun for everyone (myself included)?

Even the most dedicated photographers would, at times, rather stick bamboo shoots under their fingernails than organize a group photo. "Yes, you have to!" "Timmy, where are you? I can't see your face." "Stop squinting!" "Hey, you in the back, stop talking and smile, (explicative)!" These phrases are all too familiar. But, you wanna know the key to making things fun? It's all in the attitude. If you are an engaging and innovative photographer, your subjects will be all smiles!

Kelly

SUPPLIES:
Patterned papers (DieCuts with a View); chipboard accents, letter accents, rub-ons (Heidi Swapp); pen; cardstock

Don't Pose Them

Who says faces in a group shot need to be staring directly at the camera with perfect grins? For many group shots, that is darn near impossible, especially when photographing small children, says Kelly. This shot shows spunk and personality, which makes for a memorable group shot that these brothers will cherish forever.

Angle the Shot

OK, so this really might not make it more fun for those in the photo (promises of candy or money, usually works), but it will lend a cool perspective to your shot! Diana asked these three unruly teen boys to sit on a stoop. She then positioned herself at an angle to them, resulting in a shot with an interesting sense of linear perspective.

SUPPLIES:
Patterned papers (EK Success, K & Co.); letter stickers (Rusty Pickle); chipboard accents (Heidi Swapp); gaffer tape, page reinforcements, date sticker, (7 Gypsies); twill tape (Scenic Route Paper Co.); rub-ons (Creative Imaginations); acrylic paint; pen; font (www.P22.com)

Diana H.

BUILDING A HOME PHOTO STUDIO
Transform a corner, backyard or garage into a temporary portrait studio

Creating a home studio will allow you to take professional-quality portraits. You just need a little bit of space, some nice light and a few odds and ends. Oh, and don't forget a willing photo subject.

Find the space | The ideal space for a home studio is one with lots of natural light and that is large enough to accommodate a backdrop, set up props and allow at least three feet of space between you and the subject. We recommend considering your garage, a well-lit corner of the living room or a porch.

Find the light | The space you choose for your home studio must receive natural light. Look for spots that are close to large windows or doors. The garage is ideal because, with the garage door open, it will receive a large amount of soft light. If the light is too direct, use a curtain or large leafy plant to filter it. North-facing windows are best during the early morning or late afternoon. If you don't have a space with natural light, consider purchasing clamp lights (purchase at the hardware store) or photo lamps to supplement the existing light.

Buy the equipment | You'll need to make only a small investment in your home studio. First, buy a few sheets to use as backdrops. White or black are always solid choices, but also try pastel colors to highlight skins tones or match with eye color. A reflector is also a sound investment. A reflector will help you to evenly light your subject. You can use a white sheet, solid piece of white foam core or purchase a professional-quality reflector. You may also want to buy a stool for subjects to sit on or for you to stand on while snapping photos.

When traveling, what are some tips for photographing the sites?

Nothing says "tourist!" like a big ol' camera dangling from your neck, but hey, you're a scrapbooker, so embrace the role. Consistency in image quality is going to be your biggest challenge when you travel. You're snapping photos all day, therefore you're at the mercy of the constantly changing lighting conditions. Lugging the camera and all the accompanying gear and supplies is draining. Just remember to have fun and, when time and film supply permits, to take several shots, experimenting with flash/no flash, orientation and image composition.

Capture a Golden Glow

Sunset is one of the best times to take photos. The light quality is rich and warm, casting a golden glow on everything it touches. Susan was lucky enough to be at a prime vantage point at sunset while on a trip to Mexico. Dawn is an equally nice time to capture glorious photos, but we understand that vacations aren't usually about being a morning person.

SUPPLIES:
Patterned paper, brads (American Crafts); fabric letter accents (Scrapworks); cardstock; brads

Susan W.

Seek Images That Move You

Travelers can become so preoccupied with getting photos of landmarks and grand vistas that the little things escape them. Heidi recommends narrowing your view to capture images of the tiny details that strike a chord. "I try to take photos of something that moved me emotionally," she says. "Look for architectural designs that inspire you, children wearing different styles of clothing or playing games that are foreign to you. Even photograph different foods you've tried!" For this layout, Heidi scrapbooked a photo of a boutique display window that was located just across the street from her hotel in Paris. The support image shows the inside view of her hotel window. These are images that whisk her back to Paris, she says.

SUPPLIES:
Patterned paper (FMI); ribbon (Michael's); air-dry modeling compound; stamping ink; buttons (Magic Scraps, Die Cuts With a View); fonts (Black Jack, Wade Sans Light)

Heidi

Zoom In for Detail

"One thing I like to do whenever I travel is to keep a look out for big differences and small details," Trudy says. While in Manchester, England, she came across this stream that ran through seemingly a million bits and pieces of slate. She zoomed in to capture the intricate detail of the stream but was also sure to snap a photo of the area in which it was located, which she included on the scrapbook page to give the focal image context.

SUPPLIES:
Patterned paper (FontWerks); cardstock; brads (Bazzill); chipboard letters (Heidi Swapp); date stamp (Just Rite Stamps); photo turns (7 Gypsies); stamping ink; acrylic paint; foam adhesive; font (Arial)

manchester ROCKS

One of the days during our stay in Manchester, Sally took Dad and the kids I and downtown to Shambles Square, the area that was bombed on June 15th 1996 by the IRA. The "Old Wellington" and "Sinclair's Oyster Bar" (in the photo below) are the oldest buildings in Manchester City and were moved 100 yards when the area, and new Shambles Square, was rebuilt. Right opposite (and where I was standing to take this photo) was an outdoor amphitheater built into the sloping ground. We were there the day of the World Cup and there was a huge screen displaying the England vs. Germany football match. At the top of the amphitheater was the coolest slate stone "stream" that was 6 or more feet wide and went longer than I can remember. I don't know if you were allowed to stand on it or not, but I just couldn't help myself so that I could get this fantastic abstract shot. I love this great city!

Trudy

6/02/02

When it comes to capturing candids, subtlety is not exactly my strong suit. How can I snap photos on the sly?

Two words: telephoto lens. If you have an SLR camera equipped with this guy or a digital with a super-powerful zoom lens, you can position yourself at a distance from your subject and snap photos inconspicuously. Combine this with fast-speed film (ISO 800 or higher) and you can take photos in rapid-fire succession, which will increase the likelihood of an exceptional candid image. Or, take a cue from the paparazzi by hiding in the bushes or doggedly tailing your photo subjects—just don't hold us accountable for any ensuing altercations.

Shoot From Afar

"I feel like the paparazzi! Stalking my kids with a zoom lens," Kelli admits. At least she's not selling the photos to gossip rags. For this totally in-the-moment photo, Kelli was pretty far from the action, making her (and her camera's zoom lens) presence virtually unknown. Because the tykes were so immersed in fun, they had no idea they were being photographed for inquiring minds the world over to see.

SUPPLIES:
Patterned papers (Carolee's Creations);
die-cut letters (QuicKutz); stamping ink; cardstock

Kelli

"My husband came home one day to find his tall ladder propped against the garage. He just shook his head when I told him I got it out so I could take pictures of the boys playing basketball from ABOVE the basket!"
Kelli

higher! HIGHER!!

An older cousin
And a boy of four
One pushing higher
One calling for more.

Get Behind the Action

With respect to people's hang-ups about their backsides, photos taken from this perspective can capture poignant moments of emotion. From behind, you can capture linked arms, touching heads, facial profiles engaged in eye contact. "I took this photo at my cousin's wedding," Susan says, "while he and his wife had no idea that I was behind them snapping it. This turned out to be one of my favorite shots from their wedding."

SUPPLIES:
Patterned paper (7 Gypsies, FiberMark); cardstock; ribbon, brads (American Crafts); rub-on (K & Co.); rhinestone (Westrim); metal embellishment (Nunn Designs)

{D & R} On the Brink of Forever

LOVE

), one who loves
affection lovely

May they only find much happiness,
And an abundance of blessings,
In their future together. (photo 5.2005)

Susan W.

Focus First and Wait

Suzy

A successful predator planning a surprise attack on her prey never underestimates the power of patience. When it comes to surprise photo attacks on her children, Suzy is a master of this tactic. Here, she caught her daughter just as she was popping up from behind a playground structure. The trick: anticipate the area of action, focus your camera on that spot and…wait with a ready trigger finger. When trying this on your own children, Suzy advises, "Just take the picture before they have time to respond."

SUPPLIES:
Patterned paper (K & Co., Sandylion Sticker Designs); rhinestones (Darice, Making Memories); letter accents (Heidi Swapp); buttons (Making Memories); felt; pens; embroidery floss

"The magic of the Garden Isle is calling me back home."

This photo of Chloe takes me back to Kauai. Her hair so softly blowing, the relaxed look on her face. Hawaiian flowers in the background all remind me of our Garden Isle Vacation.

There's a place I recall Not too big, in fact it's kind of small. The people there say they got it all - the simple life for me! Hele on to Kauai Hanalei by the bay. Wailua River Valley is where I used to play. The canyons of Waimea standing all alone. The magic of the garden Isle is calling me back home.

July, 2005

Garden Girl

What's all this jazz about "perspective" in photography? How can I use it to my advantage?

Imagine if your neck were immobile. You wouldn't be able to look from side to side or cock your head to look up and around or even look down. If you were only able to look straight ahead, your visual life would be pretty boring and uninformative. Now, relate this thought to your photography. Photos needn't and shouldn't always be taken from one vantage point. When composing a shot, look at it from all angles—which angle will provide the most telling perspective? One from above, below, the side, far away, close up or straight on?

SUPPLIES:
Patterned paper (KI Memories); star accents, chipboard accents (Heidi Swapp); letter stickers (Making Memories); pen; cardstock

Joanna

Height and Motion

If life were only always this carefree. This page captures a boy's first springtime swing time. Joanna wanted to convey the proverbial "higher! higher!" demands from swing-set-addicted children. She composed these photos inside a tight frame to eliminate background distraction. To imply height, she shot the photos while sitting on the ground (notice her son in relation to the fence in the background). She also captured the to-and-fro swinging motion by showing photos of Cole swinging away from and toward her.

Worm's-Eye View

When you want your subject to look larger than life or when you want to convey a sense of elevation, shoot pictures with a worm's-eye view—meaning, position yourself beneath your subject and shoot in an upward direction. Vanessa asked her daughter and daughter's friends to climb to the top of the slide at a playground. Vanessa perched herself at the bottom and composed this playful shot. Worm's-eye views are also great for shooting smaller photo subjects, such as babies or pets.

SUPPLIES:
Patterned paper, stickers (American Crafts); white tag (Sizzix); rub-on (My Mind's Eye); clip (Heidi Swapp); brads (American Crafts, Making Memories); cardstock; font (www.twopeasinabucket.com)

Vanessa

Rearview

Rearview shots—they're akin to being behind the scenes, in the action, ready for something to happen. For this photo, Katherine wanted to show the depth of the ramp from which her little dare-devil son was about to descend as well as the view of the BMX track in front of him. "This photograph is a representation of the subject's form and shape, and the viewer is given the sensation of volume, space, depth and distance," she says.

SUPPLIES:
Patterned paper (My Mind's Eye); letter stamps, rub-ons, letter accents (Making Memories); chipboard accents (Basic Grey); brads (Junkitz); clear gloss medium; corrugated cardboard; stamping ink

Katherine

Since the camera already adds ten pounds, what are some simple ways to flatter a photo subject?

We've all shuddered at that phrase. Now, it's time to say, "Oh yeah? Well, my photography skills will make your butt look amazing!" Photographers use a few posing tricks to flatter photo subjects. For example, when photographing females, put the shoulders at an angle toward the camera for a slimming effect. For a head shot, stand above a female, angle her head and ask her to look up. When photographing a male, square his shoulders to the camera and shoot from waist height.

Quinn

May 31, 2005

Swinging in his swing....

It is a quiet morning. Reagan is fast asleep in her bed, and you have Mommy all to yourself.

You awake and immediately take my hand and lead me to the door. From the window you can see outside, and it is clear you know

where you want to be. I oblige, turn the handle on the knob of the door, and head outside into the dew-covered yard. After a quick

glance around, you take me directly to the swing. I put you in and with a little push, you giggle as if to say, "Push me higher, Mommy."

A smile spreads wide across your face. You are content. You are happy.

Your spirit is [flying high.]

Amber

SUPPLIES:
Patterned paper (Sassafras Lass); brads, photo turns, buckle (Queen & Co.) cardstock; font (Georgia)

Use Natural Light

Bathing your photo subject in natural light is the best way to flatter him or her. Natural light reduces the appearance of blemishes and complements skin tones the best (if only it would makes us all look skinny). Outdoors, in the early morning light, Amber snapped these photos of her son in a natural state of exaltation. The boy was swinging at the time of the photo shoot, which also adds to his joyful expression.

Use a Complementary Backdrop

We could just fall inside those beautiful blue eyes. Danielle is well aware of her son's alluring baby blues and, for this photo shoot, wanted to really enhance them. She dressed Cooper in a pastel blue shirt and set him against a pastel blue background. When choosing a backdrop for your own photo shoot, ask your subject what color is most complementary for him or her. Then, select a similar color for the background that does not distract from your photo subject's features.

SUPPLIES:
Corrugated cardboard (Westrim); button (Autumn Leaves); embroidery floss; letter stickers (American Crafts, Autumn Leaves, Making Memories); pen; dimensional paint; stamping ink; felt; fabric; notebook paper; acrylic paint

Danielle

Expert Advice!

Ways to relax a photo subject:

* Make sure the subject is well fed and rested.
* Photograph the subject at the time of day when she is most happy.
* Engage her in conversation.
* Allow her to lean against something.
* Photograph her with a favorite toy or object.

Convert to Black-and-White

You could have a photograph of your child covered head to toe in mud, and if you printed it in black-and-white, viewers would ooh and awe at its "artistic beauty." Black-and-white photos have an innate classic quality to them. For this photo, Susan composed the shot so that the contemporary vase would be bathed in natural light. Using her image-editing software, she converted the image to black-and-white.

SUPPLIES:
Patterned paper (KI Memories); ribbon, letter stickers (American Crafts); brads (Creative Imaginations); cardstock

Susan W.

When I scrapbook my old Polaroids, I feel like my pages look as dated as my mother's beehive hairdo. Help!

For some, the creative genius behind a successful Polariod-packed layout is as elusive as the wherewithal to solve a Rubik's Cube. Polaroids and other photos from days of yore keep scrapbookers scratching their heads because of their odd shape, discoloration and less-than-amazing image composition. Our solution is to view these drawbacks as charming attributes. If you can't beat 'em, play 'em up for sweet nostalgia and humor.

Shannon

PHOTO: JONATHON BURKS

SUPPLIES:
Patterned paper (Me & My Big Ideas); brads, buttons (Junkitz); paper flowers (Prima); cardstock; rickrack, lettering (source unknown)

Find Patterns in the Photo

Embrace the garishness, in all its glory! That is Shannon's advice for working with '70s photos. The butterfly and daisy motif seen on the highchair inspired her own motif choices. As for the colors—"The '70s were gaudy, so use them all," she says.

Give Them Funky Mats

To scrapbook these vintage '60s photos, Jennifer traveled back in time. "I like to keep the design similar to the era," she says. "I went back to the old-school style of scrapping with the pieced flowers." Rather than cropping the photos, she highlighted them with big, funky mats. To draw attention to the top left photo, she matted it on top of a large chipboard circle, which she had painted yellow.

SUPPLIES:
Circle punches (Creative Memories); photo turns (Junkitz); chipboard; brads (SEI); acrylic paint; pencil eraser (used as a stamp); cardstock; font (Flamenco)

Jennifer B.

The other day, Mom and I, were looking through some old pictures when we came across these two. I just adore seeing Mom and Dad so young and so in love! These pictures were taken during their first year of courtship around 1969. Mom was still a senior in high school and Dad had been in the Air Force for a little over a year at this point. They have been through so much during these last 37 years and I am happy to report that they are still in love to this day! Journaling 03-19-2006

Digitally Enhance

This image has issues. Not only is it an odd shape, full of funky colors and patterns (by the way, nice pants, Valerie!), the image quality is poor. Valerie enlarged the image and performed a little color correction to brighten the colors. She also played with the contrast to ease the shadowy edges. The original photo anchors the title. "I wanted to keep the original photo so my kids could see what older photos look like," Valerie says.

SUPPLIES:
Patterned paper (Scenic Route Paper Co.); fabric tabs (Scrapworks); letter stickers (Miss Elizabeth's); frame (Li'l Davis Designs); pen

Valerie B.

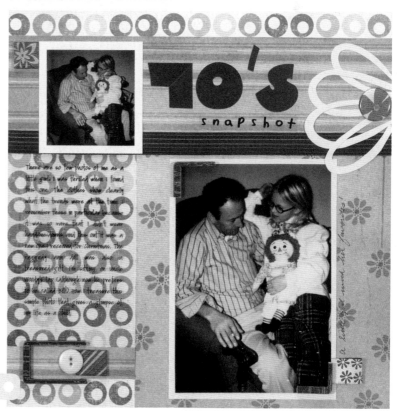

What are three way-cool digital photo effects?

Point. Click. Alter. Most digital photo effects are so easy that even the writer of this book could accomplish them if only she weren't plagued with that darn technology anxiety. Seriously, digital photo effects are easy. If you always remember to work with duplicate images (save the originals as backups), you can freely and safely experiment. Here, we've shown you just a few of the awesome digital things that can be done to photos. Your computer is waiting to show you more.

Your first close inspection of a flower revealed that each is unique, and beautiful to see and touch. Then you put it in your mouth, bit down, and quickly found that sometimes a beautiful sight doesn't equal great flavor. Ah discovery. (And a good thing Nilla Wafers mask the daisy aftertaste. Something to remember.)

SUPPLIES:
Patterned paper, rub-ons (Basic Grey, KI Memories); cardstock

Jessica

Spot Color

Digital photo-tinting, or adding spot color, can be subtle or dramatic. Jessica's approach is both. She added spot color to the focal photo to help draw attention to it. For the layout, she created duplicate black-and-white images of the original color photos. To add the spot color to the focal photo, she layered the black-and-white duplicate image on top of the original color image. Using the small eraser brush, she carefully erased around the flower on the black-and-white layer, which reveals the vibrant color beneath. Merge the two layers and print the photo.

Kelli

A Soft Blur

Just like the saying, "Behind every good writer is a good editor," behind every good photo is a good image editor. This beautiful portrait was given a soft touch by Kelli. She desaturated the photo, which also enhanced the brown tones of the photo. To achieve what Kelli called the "dreamy feel" of the photo, she applied soft light action. Finally, she used the layers function within the software to add the handsomely scripted text to the image.

SUPPLIES:
Textured paper (Mulberry Invitations); frame, photo corners (EK Success); letter dies (QuicKutz); stamping ink; ribbon, lace, velvet paper (source unknown); vintage jewelry

Expert Advice!

Some tips when using digital techniques:

* When altering photographs, always work on duplicate images. That way, if you make a mistake, you still have the original.

* When naming digital files, be consistent and thorough. For example, list a basic theme, small detail and date (e.g., xmas_2004_dinner).

A Digital Border

Caught by the striking simplicity of abundance and joy in this photo, Jenn did just a few things to enhance it. First, she converted the color image to black-and-white. She used the "curves" and "channel mixing" features within her image-editing software to achieve the pinkish-grey color of the photo. To really draw the eye, she added the distressed digital photo border.

SUPPLIES:
Patterned digital paper (www.shabbyprincess.com); digital border (blairblanks.com); image-editing software

Jenn B.

Why is it so hard to remember this? Why does it take weeks of planning, hours of packing, tons of shopping, loads of organizing to remember that the most fun things are the easiest.

The feeling of the Florida breeze in your hair. The tiny sand crystals that seep between your toes. The chance to just play and explore with no time limits.

So, with this "simple" page, I give my renewed committment. To notice the little things, everyday. To enjoy my kids and not stress about the small stuff.

To simplify my life.

life is simple. just live it.

Psst! In this chapter you will learn how to...

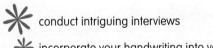

※ conduct intriguing interviews

※ incorporate your handwriting into your pages

※ create fun journaling treatments

※ write with verve

※ scrapbook for therapeutic value

※ scrapbook about yourself

※ infuse wedding pages with pizzazz

※ creatively scrapbook the holidays

※ get new ideas for birthday pages

※ find too-cool-for-school ideas for back-to-school pages

How to add verve and voice to scrapbook journaling

Journaling. It's integral to a scrapbook page. It fills in the blanks the photos cannot. It holds the names, the dates, the details. But, let's be honest. It can kinda stink.

"Journaling" is rooted in the word "journal," which means diary or a personal record of a person's daily life or work. It also means writing, and writing for most of us is extremely difficult. It's hard wrapping words around our emotions.

If you feel like you just can't write, at least know that you're not alone. Heck, there are probably hundreds of thousands of scrapbook pages out there without a lick of journaling on them. But those pages may suffer a fate worse than death. Without journaling, your future descendants will have no connection to the people in your scrapbooks, and they may just toss them.

We want to help save your scrapbooks and give you confidence in your journaling ability. So, flip the page and prepare to be inspired.

Whenever I interview my loved ones for my scrapbook pages, eyes tend to glaze. What are some topics that will surely keep them interested?

That's funny. Most people we know will, if given the chance, go on and on about themselves and everything else to anyone who will listen. First, make sure you're interviewing them at a convenient time. If they are too busy, too tired, too hungry, they're going to be preoccupied. Second, be subtle about it. Start by asking about their day or how it felt to hit the winning home run. Third, pay attention to what sparks their passion and go from there.

TWOSOME · UNSTOPPABLE · DYNAMIC DUO · BIRDS OF A FEATHER · BEST BUDS · INSEPARABLE

sHe SaiD:

Mama: "So Sophie, do you love Zach?"
Sophie: "No!"
Mama: "Does Zach love you?
Sophie: "Yes!" (lots of giggles!)
Mama: "How do you know Zach loves you?"
Sophie: "Cause he asked me if I wanted to sleep in his sleeping bag. His sleeping bag was so little – it was an inch big and he wanted me to sleep in there with him! He also told me he kisses girls at school. And then he said I wanna marry you Sophie! He told Thane if we got married, he would take me away. He asked Thane if he would be sad and told him we would start a new family together! He wanted to sit next to me at Ruby's too."
Mama: "Do you think he really wanted you to marry him?"
Sophie: "Ummm...yeah! Cause he acted like it!"
Mama: "Why do you think he likes you so much?"
Sophie: "Because, I don't know! He put a heart with an S in it in his journal. He let me read it." (more giggles!)
Mama: "Do you want him to come back and stay?
Sophie: "Yes, so he'll keep saying it! I think it's funny!"

He SaiD:

Jamie: "So Zack, what did you do on vacation?"
Zach: "I went to the beach and hung out with my new friends Thane, Sophie, and Chloe. Sophie is my best friend though; I thought that she was pretty cute."
Jamie: "So do you think that she is your girlfriend?"
Zach: "No way, just my friend that I think is cute. Oh and I asked her to marry me. She said no, but that is because we are too young right now, that is why we are just friends. But we will get married when we are old enough."
Jamie: "When will that be?"
Zach: "Like when we are 16 we will get married."
Jamie: "But I thought that you said you were just friends?"
Zach: "Well you always say that you married your best friend, and Sophie is mine, so that's why I KNOW we are getting married. Yup, I'm marrying my cutest, bestest friend. I can't wait to see her this summer, and don't worry mom, I know we are still little, so she is just still my friend."

together is a wonderful place to be

FiRsT PRoPOSaL

OPEN

Suzy

SUPPLIES:
Patterned papers (Sandylion Sticker Designs); letter stickers (Sandylion Sticker Designs, Basic Grey); transparency; pen

Relationships

Innocent youths have such a black-and-white perspective when it comes to the complexities of relationships. Suzy's daughter received a sweet proposal from a close friend. For the scrapbook page, Suzy details her daughter's version of the story as well as the friend's. By using their own words, Suzy's journaling brims with personality and excitement.

Word Associations

If you really want to know what's happening between the ears of a loved one, give them a word association test. Just be warned: You may never look at this person the same again. Over lunch one day, Jodi gave Torrey this simple test. "This technique is fun and casual, too," Jodi says, "and will often result in unexpected answers." Whenever Torrey drew a blank, she would simply answer, "green." Jodi decided to highlight those answers in, well, green! Jodi printed the words and answers onto cardstock to use as the background of this page.

SUPPLIES:
Cardstock; flowers (Prima); rhinestones (Me and My Big Ideas); die-cut letters (QuicKutz); decorative scissors (Fiskars); dimensional paint; rubber stamp (PSX Design); stamping ink

Jodi A.

a trip to left field

black blue • white green • sunshine rain • mountain stream • fishing flies • table chair • water ice • create einstein • magic johnson • sketch bar • crayon rainbow • photo opportunity • play mold • artist mom • family love • quiet snore • seashore shells • ocean serenity • chocolate yum • potato potato • jewel mile • sand which • question mark • writing reading • books scotty • become transform • girl boy • pink green • walk chinese • play ground • game poker • fashion sense • inspire blank • color bright • excite bright • explore scuba diver • great dane • world wide • memories making • watermelon spit • rest weary • relax renew • solitude alone • warm cold • vital organs • wish blow • marsh mellow

adventure unknown • baby soft • pig blanket • welcome mat • purse pig's ear • identity clause • intelligent green • love all • finale beat • quote saying • journal blood • reality check • style unique • emotion sleeve • quick dead • crush orange • hour minute • field left • green kermit • expression saying

stamp imported • dirt mud • computer genius • light camera • drink merry • bound gagged • best worst • simple simon • talent tap dancing • patient virtue • friendship job • paris france • thought process • group hug • chicken lips • fear factor • funny laugh • fanatic survivor • digital camera • legacy sorority

monday green • church pew • follow leader • talk incessantly • brick mortar • drive insane • bicycle cards • horse buggy • found object • clear soap • calm peaceful • think alike • sense ability • feel touchy • mood pms • liver chicken • foot mouth • car go • reach green • give take

help need • important document • number cruncher • permission slip • repair green • subject title • secret whisper • deadline wednesday • ultimate uber • inspiration job • amazing grace • master baiter • essential necessary • guide follow • obsessed cat • focus blurry • variety spice • word association • long chinaman • invent create

win lose • fame fortune • honor offer • day night • song south • right wrong • youth wasted • fabulous sassy • analize critical • roll punches • demand ask • encourage green • finger heidi • proof pudding • stuff junk • fantasy island • difficult this • humor laugh • forget green

beautiful bejeweled • fun frolic • sport team • couch potato • bed messy • shower a day • fairytale ending • story chapter • princess bride • frog prince • fish hook • glass break • beef where's • food full • survive strong • mentor einstein • teacher papa • sour sweet • opportunity knock • colorado home • cat cosmo • dog cosmo • hot cold • tree christmas • blossom bloom • fresh funky • dream peaceful • believe faith • wisdom knowledge • bra boobs • smart me • fat me • knowledge apple • socks shoes • hike football • choice freedom • leather lace • tear fear • weak strong • trouble job • work play • rob green • square circle • object affection • favorite best • salty sweet • bird hand

---

Occupations

"What do you do?" It's a simple question that will open up a field of conversation possibilities. Here, Diana asked her friend about being a teacher. She angled the interview to focus on what it is like for a teacher on the first day of school each year. This interview was conducted via e-mail, but her friend decided to write the responses onto notebook paper. Diana used the written answers because the lined notebook paper fit so well with the page theme.

SUPPLIES:
Patterned paper, rub-on (Making Memories); chipboard accents, stickers (KI Memories); frame (Heidi Swapp); stickers (Pebbles)

Diana G.

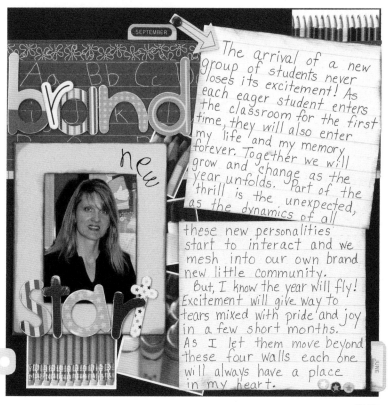

The arrival of a new group of students never loses its excitement! As each eager student enters the classroom for the first time, they will also enter my life and my memory forever. Together we will grow and change as the year unfolds. Part of the thrill is the unexpected, as the dynamics of all these new personalities start to interact and we mesh into our own brand new little community. But, I know the year will fly! Excitement will give way to tears mixed with pride and joy in a few short months. As I let them move beyond these four walls each one will always have a place in my heart.

I know it's important to include my handwriting on my layouts, but my penmanship is awful. Are there less obvious ways to include it?

"Your handwriting is your personal stamp, and it says a lot about you." Yeah, sure, whatever. The best reason to include your handwriting, no matter how terrible you think it is, is that kiddos and family will appreciate it. Would it kill you to add a handwritten date or simple love note? It's not like you have to write out the entire journaling block (because you are journaling, aren't you?).

Joanna

SUPPLIES:
Patterned papers (Chatterbox); chipboard letters (Heidi Swapp); chipboard hearts (Imagination Project); thread; image-editing software

Scan It

If you are hesitant to include your handwriting on a layout, Joanna feels your pain. But for her, it's more a matter of making a mistake than being ashamed of her penmanship. The genius that she is, though, Joanna has found a remedy: Scan the handwriting and then print it directly on an enlarged photo. "By scanning it, I can manipulate the size, correct mistakes and rearrange or straighten lines of text," she says. This technique also allows her to see the handwriting as a design element rather than her "bumping, bumbling words," she says.

Use in Small Doses

When it comes to including handwriting on a layout, Heidi has a no-fail formula: a little handwriting + fonts, letter stickers and lettering templates = tidy pages with a personal touch. For this layout, Heidi handwrote the tags used to detail this rambunctious photo series. She also included some handwritten words in the otherwise computer-printed journaling block. "If I can manage it, I sometimes work in a secret message with my handwritten words," Heidi says. Did she manage to do that this time? Take a look at the journaling block to see.

SUPPLIES:
Patterned paper (Black Round); brads (Making Memories, Joann Stores); letter stickers (Chatterbos, FMI); wooden frame (Chatterbox); rub-on, pin (Around the Block); ribbon (Michaels); lettering template (The Crafter's Workshop); font (Wolf print)

Heidi

Cleverly Disguise It

The swirling lines of Kelly's hand-scripted captions look more like design elements than examples of her handwriting. "I used my handwriting as the stems and leaves of the flowers," she says. "It became a free-floating design to be seen as an element of my page rather than what it said or how it was written."

Kelly

SUPPLIES:
Cardstock; plastic flowers (Heidi Swapp, Queen & Co.); brads (Queen & Co.); ribbon (Offray); rickrack (Doodlebug Design, SEI); tag (Sizzix); letter stickers (Doodlebug Design); pen

I'm not a fan of paragraph-style journaling. What are my options?

Don't fancy yourself as a writer, eh? That's OK. It's enough that you actually want to include the journaling. As long as the journaling describes, emotes or states facts, it's really not important that it appears as part of a well-scripted paragraph or even in subject/predicate form (that's a fancy way of saying "sentence"). Sprinkle the page with descriptive words, use a bullet-pointed list. Just put a few words on the page so the full memory is preserved.

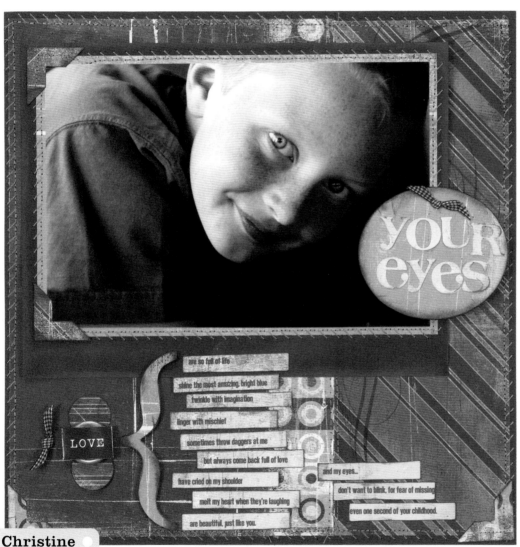

SUPPLIES:
Patterned papers, stickers (Basic-Grey); chipboard accents (Bazzill); ribbon (Michael's); corner punch (EK Success); metal hardware (Basic Grey, Pebbles); stamping ink; cardstock

Christine

Journaling Strips

This technique requires that you follow just two rules from English class: Be descriptive and use parallel construction. For this page, Christine wanted to focus on the beauty and soulfulness of her son's eyes. The journaling, which is a list of descriptive phrases, reads as an extension of the title. Notice how each phrase begins with a present-tense verb—that's an excellent example of parallel construction (constructing a series of phrases with identical syntax). It provides a cohesive flow and rhythmic pacing for the journaling.

March 1
Left CDA in the Suburban at
4:30 p.m.

March 2
Arrived in San Diego at
Grandmother's house at 5 p.m.

March 3
Barbeque on the beach with
Daniel & Lynn's wedding guests

March 4
Daniel & Lynn's Wedding

March 5
Grandmother, Sheila & Samantha
did some shopping while Joel,
Rebekah, Lucas & Tyler visited Don,
Karen, Nathan & Emily

March 6
Took all the kids & Catherine to
Sea World for the day

March 7
Left San Diego for Phoenix.
Stopped at the dinosaurs in
Indio on the way

March 8
Family Fun Center with
Shannon's kids. Shannon &
Sheila had a "Mom's Night Out"
together

March 9
Trip to the Phoenix Zoo with
Shannon's family

March 10
A day to rest. Joel watched older
kids while Shannon, Sheila & the
babies went to Target

March 11
Said goodbye to Shannon's family
& started the trip home at 8:45 a.m.

March 12
After a Suburban breakdown a
mile from home, arrived at the
house at 11 a.m.

Southwest Vacation

Sheila

Calendar-Style

Calendars help us keep track of our lives, so they lend themselves well to journaling that's full of detail. Sheila needed a way to capture a week's worth of activities on one page. Using image-editing software, she created a photo montage full of representative detail. To the left of it, she added a journaled column that succinctly details the events of each vacation day. Sheila altered the colors of the dates for punch.

SUPPLIES:
Patterned papers (American Crafts); cardstock; photo paper; Adobe Photoshop image-editing software; font (Century Gothic)

Simple Sentences

Why be a chatty Cathy when being a woman of few words will suffice? Valerie makes a graceful statement with this mini album. The images are so compelling, they needed only a simple descriptive statement. Valerie handwrote each statement and cut them into strips. She placed them in the album so that they would naturally lead the eye to the photos. For extra pop, she used distressed letter stickers to begin each statement.

SUPPLIES:
Patterned papers (Scenic Route Paper Co.); fibers (Basic Grey); frame (Li'l Davis Designs); stickers (Pebble, Inc.); pen

Valerie B.

JUST THE FACTS
Be sure to include these essentials in your journaling.

Who | Who is in the photo? Who was also there but not in the photo?

What | What is going on in the photo? What happened before and after the photo was taken?

Where | Where did the memory take place?

When | What time of day was it? What was the date? Be sure to include the year.

Why | Why was this even so scrapbook-worthy? Why is it taking place?

How | How did the memory come to be?

For some pages, the journaling is very personal. How can I discreetly include it?

The therapeutic power of journaling should never be underestimated. Scrapbooking about personal challenges takes great strength, and the emotional rewards to be reaped from doing so are just as strong. If you have hardships that you would like to scrapbook, but are wary of the scrapbook pages being viewed, consider creating a personal scrapbook for only you to look at and reflect upon.

Photo Flip-Up

Nic designed this layout so that it would appear to have no journaling at all. The journaling is discreetly hidden behind the photo. It details Nic's feelings about the cycle of life after a miscarriage. To create the flip mechanism, Nic attached the photo to the background with small, barely-there hinges.

SUPPLIES:
Patterned paper (BasicGrey, Scenic Route Paper Co.); rhinestones (Making Memories); fabric, hinges, ribbon (unknown source); chipboard accents (Maya Road); rub-ons (Basic Grey); cardstock; stamping ink

40

Hide a Booklet

When you have a story to tell, but don't wish to wear it on your sleeve, a hidden journaling booklet is an excellent choice. Shannon created this page to tell the story of how one devoted mother passed on a nurturing spirit to two sisters, who as adults, shared a dream of motherhood. The story winds to detail the trials Shannon's sister endured while trying to become pregnant. Shannon tucked the four-page booklet behind the focal photo, which she adhered to the page with foam adhesive to allow room for the booklet. On the booklet binding, Shannon attached ribbon with brads—the extra depth prevents the booklet from completely sliding beneath the photo.

SUPPLIES:
Patterned paper (Sandylion Sticker Designs); rub-ons (Making Memories); ribbon (American Crafts); rubble, sequins (Magic Scraps); frame (Pebbles); brads (Junkitz, Pebbles); cardstock; glaze

Shannon

For those who are lucky enough to experience motherhood first hand, each day is an adventure in love & acceptance. Trials & tribulations can be easily forgotten when a child looks into his mother's eyes and for the first time says "Momma" with that teeny tiny voice. There is no other job in the world that brings such satisfaction. From early on, my sister & I knew this was our path in life. We even had our children's names picked out before we had husbands. Way before I know for myself, motherhood couldn't come soon enough. I like to k that this urge for children is due rge part to our mother's incredible ch..d-rearing. I fondly recall Mom's

DIGGING DEEP
Get in touch with your soul with these tips and ponder points.

Write a letter | When the words won't seem to flow, try penning a letter to a loved one or to yourself. Letters have built-in starting points ("Dear Self") that will help warm the ice.

Listen to music | Make some time, grab some headphones and just sit and listen to your favorite songs. Create a mix CD of songs that might help you make sense of some of the issues with which you are wrestling.

Find quotes | Jump on Google.com and search for quotes. Other people's words may resonate with you and create a spark.

Call a friend | If you feel comfortable talking about an issue with a friend, call a close companion and just start talking. This verbal communication will help you process your thoughts.

Journal | If you are too shy to create a scrapbook page about your challenge, start first with a journal. In the journal, you can begin writing about your feelings and even add images or collage art to accompany the words. Keep the journal in a private place and only share when you're ready.

What are some writing techniques that will enliven my journaling?

Show! Don't tell! Can you hear that proverbial command from every English teacher this side of the prime meridian echo in your mind? It's dead-on true. If you want to take readers for a ride, put them in the car, show them exactly where the seatbelt is, punch the pedal to the floor and paint a picture of the scenery. Imagery, dialogue, humor, structured plots, character development, anecdotes. These are all devices that will help you infuse your journaling with life.

amusing musings at 3

Sophie: "Mommy, you know that man in the sky?"
Me: "You mean God?"
Sophie: "Yeah, God."
Me: "What about him?"
Sophie: "What's his middle name?"

2.2006

Scene: Sophie sees a rotund man walk out of a Shop in St. Armand's Circle.
Sophie: "Mommy, that man almost had a baby."
Me: "Why do you say that?"
Sophie: "Because his belly is big."

3.2006

Sophie: "Who doesn't have a daddy?"
Shak: "Lots of people don't have daddies. My daddy Passed on so I don't have a daddy anymore."
Sophie: "Next your mommy is going to die. Then you Can buy a new mommy and daddy."

3.2006

Photo 11.2005

Lisa V.

SUPPLIES:
Patterned paper (Imagination Project, Making Memories, Paper House Productions); letters (American Crafts, Scenic Route Paper Co.); flowers (Queen & Co.); rhinestones (Me and My Big Ideas); pen

Include Dialogue

Before scrapbooking, growing children only had to endure their parents' spoken memories of the funny things they said. Now, these musings are forever preserved (and even published!) on scrapbook pages. On this page, Lisa included three gems that exemplify her daughter's adorable logic. About them she says: "Listing them briefly and sequentially on a layout, they almost appear as jokes."

Use Comparisons

The fairest. The best at sports. The smartest. While comparison pages certainly can serve as a measuring stick, they are more entertaining as a record of how people are alike and different. Danielle created this page to show what she, her husband and son were all like at age two-and-a-half. She included photos of all three, which she says allows readers to see who her son resembles the most.

SUPPLIES:
Wool felt, rhinestones (Westrim); chipboard letters (Making Memories); floss (DMC); decorative applique (Autumn Leaves); crocheted square (www.UrbanArtsandCrafts.com); ribbon (Li'l Davis Designs); cardstock; stamping ink; pen

Danielle

Cartoon Bubbles

If only we knew what our photo subjects were thinking! By using cartoon bubbles, we can intimate what we think they are thinking, and often the result is journaling touched by humor. On this page, Vanessa wrote the journaling from her dog's perspective, who was probably none too thrilled to be dressed in a pink sweatshirt and tutu for a photo shoot. But, Vanessa rationalizes that the dog had her eyes on the prize—a treat!

SUPPLIES:
Patterned paper (Doodlebug Design); paper flowers (Prima); rhinestones (EK Success); cardstock; pen; font (www.twopeasinabucket.com)

Vanessa

Scrapbooking has such therapeutic value. What are some ways to use scrapbooking to help myself and others feel better about ourselves?

First of all, we just want you to know that, dear reader, you rock. And your loved ones? They rock, too! See, making you and your loved ones feel special is that easy. There are tons of ways to say "I love/appreciate/need/cherish you" with a scrapbook page. Simply spend some time meditating about why you love/appreciate/need/cherish a special someone, write it down and then create a scrapbook page that complements the tone of your sentiment.

Angelia

SUPPLIES:
Patterned paper, circle letters, paperclip, rub-ons (K & Co.); rhinestone brads (Making Memories); chipboard accents, ghost letters (Heidi Swapp); acrylic accents; paper flowers (Prima)

Create a Tribute

Is there someone in your life that you adore and depend on, but maybe you've never told as much? Share your feelings by creating a special tribute page for him or her. Angelia created this page in honor of her sister, who she says in the journaling will "support anyone who needs a hand." Angelia also makes a point to emphasize her sister's devotion to God, her family and her friends. The feminine page style speaks to her sister's warmth and gentleness.

Count Your Blessings

Julie knows all too well how, in a matter of minutes, life can be changed forever. This page places a life-changing event into the context of time. When Julie was pregnant with her son, her husband was involved in an explosion at work. That day, Julie's life began to happen in five-minute increments. The pacing of the journaling relates the uncertainty and fear that Julie felt during that day and throughout her husband's recovery. It also relates the patience and gratitude she observed during his recovery.

SUPPLIES:
Patterned paper, tags (BasicGrey); number accents, rub-ons (EK Success); ribbon (Making Memories); brads (Bazzill); clear gloss medium

Julie

"This album will do the talking (and hugging) for me," says Denise of this "Just in Case" album she created for her son. Each page reminds him to always remember he is loved, even when the world gets him down. Inside is filled with bits of wisdom including the one that reminds Trent that "just in case he has a bad (basketball game), to remember he was playing for fun long before he became competitive."

SUPPLIES:
Patterned papers (Rusty Pickle, BasicGrey); stamps, buttons, metal corners (Making Memories); mesh; brads, rub-ons (Rusty Pickle); buttons (Junkitz); acrylic accents (Paper Studio); charms; staples; gold leafing; embellishments (JewelCraft, Boutique Trims, Darice); ribbon (Offray); stamping ink; foam adhesive; font (Carbon Copy)

Remember the Good Things

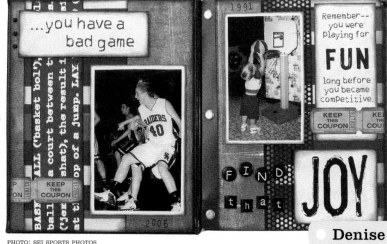

PHOTO: SEI SPORTS PHOTOS

Denise

I have discovered that life truly is all about me, so what are some creative ways to scrapbook about myself?

Congratulations on such a profound and happy revelation! Yeah, to heck with the family, let's scrapbook about ourselves! As scrapbookers, sometimes we neglect ourselves and our own memories for the sake of preserving the good life for our loved ones. Try to make it a habit to create a page every once in a while for you and about you. Your loved ones will cherish them just as much as (if not more than) the pages you create for and about them.

SEEN

There are some things you can tell by looking ...

* ✳ I love the crispness of button-down shirts.
* ✳ I am a big fan of good hair products.
* ✳ Yeah, I've had dental work done.
* ✳ I'm not that adventurous when it comes to clothing.
* ✳ I love a jacket to top off an out fit (and to hide a tummy).
* ✳ I inherited my dad's green eyes.
* ✳ I have two tattoos.
* ✳ I have hands that are used to working.
* ✳ I am a jewelry wimp.
* ✳ I think being clean and well put together helps my mood.
* ✳ I love to smile and laugh (and talk!)
* ✳ I love wide-leg pants (for their slimming effect).
* ✳ I have a very expressive face.
* ✳ I think glasses are a fashion statement.
* ✳ I'm behind my camera A LOT.

And some things you can't. **unseen**

I love Diet Mt. Dew ✳ I am a geek, married to a geek ✳ I miss the mountains of the West I taught capoeira for three years ✳ I have a degree in English ✳ I served a mission in Detroit ✳ I would stay up a lot later if I didn't have kids ✳ I am a stay-home mama by choice I think integrity is the greatest virtue ✳ I love reading fantasy and science fiction ✳ I have a serious weakness for patterned paper ✳ I like to sleep on a soft, flat pillow ✳ I do freelance web design on the side ✳ I own a bright red couch ✳ I love playing World of Warcraft with my husband I get midafternoon lag at 2 pm every day ✳ I love making people laugh ✳ My dream house has hardwood floors in it - my real house doesn't ✳ I feel guilty if I sit down to watch TV (and I inherited that from my mom) ✳ Some of the best ideas I've ever had were in the shower ✳ I think Photoshop is one of life's great inventions ✳ My family makes me happy ✳ After 30 years, I finally realize that I really do like being me

Jessica

PHOTO: JARED SPRAGUE

SUPPLIES:
Patterned paper (Chatterbox); chipboard alphabet (Heidi Swapp); cardstock; fonts (Impact, www.myfonts.com)

Show Your Dualities

Jessica is a braver woman than most—she willingly journaled about her secrets and insecurities for all to see on this page. She's only stronger for it. "I wanted to create a page that highlights my qualities, both seen and unseen," she says. This page is thus divided in two—one side lists visible qualities about Jessica while the other details less obvious qualities. The divided page background also symbolizes this duality.

Pick a Favorite

We have but one word for Lisa: tease. One look at her page alerts the reader to the theme: coffee. But another look at her journaling leads the reader on—it's penned as a love letter to a "local L.A. Boy," otherwise known as her beloved coffee stop. She tells a descriptive tale of an unexpected reunion in Las Vegas as if having a cup of coffee were a sordid affair. We forgive you, Lisa, but only because you're so clever.

SUPPLIES:
Patterned paper, chipboard alphabet (K&Co.); paper flowers (Prima); brads (Making Memories); tab (Creative Imaginations); stamping ink; pen; font (Teletype)

Lisa V.

PHOTO: PAUL HOWARD

Journal Your Calling

Angie takes great pride in the fact that she has one of the most important jobs in the world—that of a loving and supportive wife and mother. "The past several years have led to many changes in my life," she says. "I have actually found that life isn't all about me. I find that I am most happy and contented when I am with my family, helping them." Therefore, she created this mini album to celebrate her role. Each family member has a page dedicated to himself and herself. Angie journals her feelings on the final page, which also features a portrait of her.

SUPPLIES:
Patterned paper, (BasicGrey); mini book (7gypsies); brads (Making Memories); rub-ons (Basic Grey, 7 Gypsies); stickers (NRN Designs); flower punch (EK Success); silk flowers; ribbon (unknown source)

Angie

I want to infuse my marriage, I mean my wedding pages, with pizzazz. Got any ideas?

Are page ideas for your wedding photos suffering that seven-year creativity itch? (Sigh.) Building the foundation of a strong wedding page takes work and imagination. It also takes patience. Maybe even a bit of humor. Actually, yes, definitely humor! When looking at your wedding photos, don't feel pressured to always create elegant and romantic pages that wax poetic about the perfectness of the day. Think about the imperfections or reflect on the surprising differences and similarities between your expectations of marriage and the reality of it.

Suzy

PHOTO: TARA WHITNEY PHOTOGRAPHY

SUPPLIES:
Textured paper (FiberMark); chipboard accents, plastic letters (Heidi Swapp); ribbon (Autumn Leaves, Making Memories, Li'l Davis Designs); alphabet stickers (Daisy D's, Creative Imaginations); ribbon rings (Li'L Davis Designs); flowers (Trim Designs); pen; rhinestones (Me and My Big Ideas); buttons (American Craft); rick rack (unknown source); pen

IF I KNEW THEN WHAT I KNOW NOW

I wouldn't have been scared to get married

I would have cherished our time before we had children

I would have relaxed and enjoyed our relationship

I would have known Tom would be a good father and provider

I wouldn't have worried about having children

I would marry Tom all over again, only sooner!

Detail Lessons Learned

Oh, if only we did know then what we know now! Many of us can relate to Suzy's sentiments. "I like to update my wedding pages with photos and journaling about how I feel currently," she says. "I think it adds an interesting perspective when you join the two worlds together." This page marks the seventh year of marriage to her husband Tom.

Use Unexpected Colors

Give yourself permission to ignore tradition when it comes to designing wedding pages. Danielle wanted to create a page that was bold, yet still romantic. Her whimsical design and punchy color scheme gush with charm. The black-and-white photos add all the elegance. The free-form design gives the reader the impression that these two share a whirlwind romance.

SUPPLIES:
Patterned paper (Anna Griffin, Autumn Leaves, K&Co., Bo-Bunny Press, Karen Foster Design); heart stamps (Hero Arts, All Night Media); brads (Making Memories); epoxy stickers (Creative Imaginations); rhinestones (Westim); rub-ons (Li'l Davis Designs); pen; chalk; mesh

Expert Advice!

More creative ideas for wedding pages:

* If I knew then what I know now.
* The seven-year itch: he said/she said.
* Less than perfect: detail the imperfections of the wedding day and how they were handled.
* Focus on the vows.

Danielle

Highlight Strange Circumstances

Shotgun weddings notwithstanding, this idea would be perfect for detailing the hijinks of a bachelor or bachelorette party, practical jokes or, as in the case of Torrey, a "surprise" wedding. Her husband-to-be didn't want the stress of a wedding to wear out his lovely lady, so he and her friends organized a surprise hand-fasting ceremony. Torrey memorialized the day with a "crime-scene" file, complete with suspects, a statement and evidence bags.

SUPPLIES:
Rubber stamps (Zettiology); file folder; paper fasteners; walnut ink; staples; pen; image-editing software; evidence labels (downloaded from internet)

Torrey

Easter eggs, holly jolly and big fat turkeys. Oh, yawn! What are some fresh ideas for holiday pages?

Is that yawn from boredom or sheer exhaustion? Any holiday packs a punch. We love them because they are filled with family, food and tradition. The photo ops are endless and amazing, but when we sit down to scrapbook the cheer, a stagnate fog can cloud our creativity. Holidays are multifaceted, which means scrapbook-worthy topics and details are abundant. These pages can be an opportunity to appreciate traditions and reflect on the past, present and future.

Easter '78

Mike and Jessica discover that the Easter Bunny is a Star Wars fan.

FAMILY

At Easter 1978 I was just 2 1/2, so I wouldn't discover until years later that "Dad" and "Easter Bunny" were synonymous. Who knew, then, that the Easter Bunny was such a big Skywalker fan? I do know that Dad took Mike to the opening of Star Wars in '77, and they shared their love for the sci-fi icon for years.

That's what makes this photo so precious to me. It's more than an Easter Bunny giving out chocolate eggs (although we got those too). It's a dad, in holiday guise, sharing with his first son a love for a great flick. As a parent now myself, I finally get it.

Journaling: March 2006

Jessica

PHOTO: BRUCE BILLS

SUPPLIES:
Patterned paper (Crate Paper); chipboard accent (Li'l Davis Designs); rub-ons (Heidi Swapp, Basic Grey); cardstock; font (Impact, Century Gothic)

Go Retro

Socks. Evidently, in Jessica's family, children can be disappointed at receiving them at more than one holiday each year. Jessica created this page not as much to commemorate the Easter of '78 as she did to memorialize a love of the movie *Star Wars* that her brother and father share. Her father had added a pair of Star Wars socks to her brother's Easter basket that year (he looks thrilled). To draw attention to the socks, Jessica added a circular design element to the corner of the photo using red brads. The chosen distressed pattern papers match the vintage colors of the heritage photo.

Focus on the Original Traditions

When Lisa flips through her Halloween scrapbook pages, she sees nothing but the proverbial kid-in-costume-looking-cute photos, trick-or-treating, school parades and classroom parties. This year, she decided to take a different route and scrapbook a funky family tradition of creating silly Halloween recipes. The resulting mini album was the perfect format for the kooky cookbook. Lisa also suggests using the idea for a hardboiled-egg recipe book for Easter.

SUPPLIES:

Patterned paper (Bo-Bunny Press, Design Originals, Rusty Pickle); dimensional stickers (EK Success); rub-ons (My Mind's Eye); ribbon (May Arts, Special Effects); beads (Blue Moon Beads); letter stamps (Hero Arts); index tabs (Avery); mini accordion file (Target); eyelets (Creative Imaginations); stamping inks; cardstock; vellum; acrylic paint; photo corners, silk flowers (source unknown); fonts (Times New Roman, www.twopeasinabucket.com)

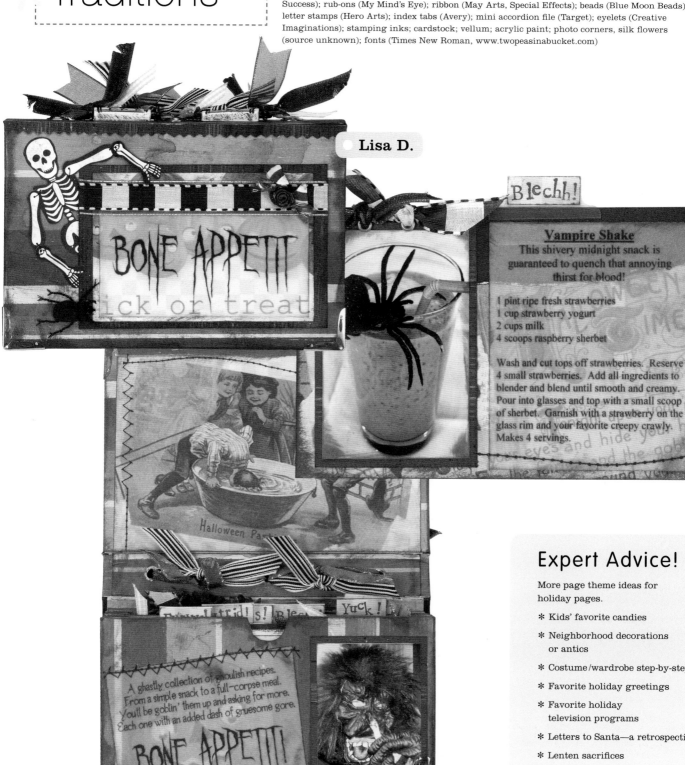

Lisa D.

Blechh!

Vampire Shake
This shivery midnight snack is guaranteed to quench that annoying thirst for blood!

1 pint ripe fresh strawberries
1 cup strawberry yogurt
2 cups milk
4 scoops raspberry sherbet

Wash and cut tops off strawberries. Reserve 4 small strawberries. Add all ingredients to blender and blend until smooth and creamy. Pour into glasses and top with a small scoop of sherbet. Garnish with a strawberry on the glass rim and your favorite creepy crawly. Makes 4 servings.

BONE APPETIT
ick or treat

Halloween Party

A ghastly collection of ghoulish recipes. From a simple snack to a full-corpse meal. You'll be goblin' them up and asking for more. Each one with an added dash of gruesome gore.

BONE APPETIT!

Expert Advice!

More page theme ideas for holiday pages.

* Kids' favorite candies

* Neighborhood decorations or antics

* Costume/wardrobe step-by-step

* Favorite holiday greetings

* Favorite holiday television programs

* Letters to Santa—a retrospective

* Lenten sacrifices

Masters, please stop the birthday clock (or at least make it less painful for me to scrapbook birthdays)!

Birthdays. They are inevitable. Birthday scrapbook pages. Also inevitable. But instead of getting frustrated by a lack of creativity, open up your mind to the creative potential of a birthday scrapbook page. Birthday pages don't always need to be about the party (although, who doesn't love a good party page?). Birthday pages can chart growth and accomplishments, reflect on dreams, honor the birthday person and more.

Chloe turns FOUR today! My little baby is no longer a baby – she is now a BIG girl! Chloe's fourth year has been so FUN; tough in some ways, but ENJOYABLE in many others! The WORDS that describe Chloe this year are: feisty, temperamental, demanding, funny, silly, outgoing, picky, loving, affectionate, charismatic, and adorable. Chloe really is a mix of SWEET and SASSY. She is either loving you and making you laugh or CRYING and complaining about something. The wonderful side of Chloe is she is the most LOVING little girl ever! She is always giving me loves and telling me how much she loves me! She loves to laugh and be SILLY. Chloe is always making us laugh. She is very FEISTY too with a strong little personality. She PLAYS so well by herself every day. She talks and makes up stories with her animals and I just listen and enjoy. I love to take WALKS with Chloe - hanging out with her is the BEST thing. Then there is the challenging side of Chloe. She is happy one minute and SCREAMING the next. She gets frustrated and mad easily and expresses it! She is very PICKY about what she wears, won't keep shoes on and hates her hair combed or anything in it. She always has HAIR in her face and is barefoot, resulting in me having to hold her a lot. Chloe always likes to be HELD and is very needy of me, day and night. I tell her she just wants to be back in my BELLY in a pouch like a baby kangaroo! She still SLEEPS with us or rather ON me and always wakes up a couple times in the night. Chloe is in a lot of TIME OUTS for hitting Sophie. When she is mad at me, she YELLS things like "I'm not sleeping with you tonight!" She started pre-school this year and tolerates it, but she would rather be HOME with me. She is so outgoing and tells girls everywhere how PRETTY they are. Even though THREE has been a bit of a challenge, we have adored every minute spent with our DARLING little girl! 03/06

Suzy

SUPPLIES:
Patterned paper (Scenic Route Paper Co.); brads (Queen & Co.); paper flowers (Making Memories, Prima); colored pencils; epoxy stickers; chipboard accents (Heidi Swapp); ribbon (source unknown)

Review the Year

The good, the bad, the ugly. It's all here in Suzy's journaling about her baby girl. Each year, on each of her children's birthdays, Suzy will write a retrospective for the previous year. "I highlight major events, accomplishments, personality traits, growth, sickness, etc.," she says. Here, she writes about her youngest daughter's feisty, sweet and sassy self.

Use a Number Theme

We recommend this technique for pages about single-digit birthdays. For this layout about her son's fourth birthday, Susan let the number four drive the theme. "I recalled the day by fours," she says. "I journaled about four things we did at his party, four things we ate, four people he invited and four gifts he received." Keeping in line with the theme, each of the four categories is represented by one photo, for a total of, yep, four.

SUPPLIES:
Metal tags, eyelet numbers, chipboard numbers (Making Memories); letter stickers (American Crafts); staples; acrylic paint; cardstock

Susan C.

Peanut butter sandwiches in letter shapes
Sub sandwiches for the adults
Potato salad
Cupcakes that you decorated yourself

4 things we ate

things we did

Baseball in the backyard
4-wheeling
Bike riding
Piñata

people you invited

Mommy and Daddy
The Lewallan family
Grannie and Papa
Aunt Carol and Uncle Chad

4 × 4

4 gifts you received

Play bowling alley Chutes and Ladders game
Thomas the Tank Engine track Puzzles

(Your fourth birthday, by fours.)

Detail the Wishes

Health, friends, happiness, grand adventure and silly fun—who wouldn't wish for that? A pre-teen girl who is more concerned with her social life, that's who. This page shows the discrepancies between a mother's heartfelt birthday wishes for her daughter and the daughter's material wants of a cell phone (maybe next year), golf cart and trampoline. Jodi kept the page fun and lighthearted with flirty patterns and a spicy color scheme. She cropped support photos to fit inside small tags for a border full of action and detail.

Jodi H.

SUPPLIES:
Patterned paper (Scenic Route Paper Co.); paper flowers (Prima); rub-ons (KI Memories); brads, bead ribbon (Joanne's); ribbon (Offray); tags (Avery); sequins (source unknown); cardstock

Wishes

Birthday Girl

My wish for you:

Your wish:

I want some too-cool-for-school ideas for back-to-school pages. Whaddya got for me?

Well now, sassy pants, you really know what you want. That's why we like you! Let's see, the start of a new school year or the first day of school for a little one is as bittersweet as it gets. We're so proud to see our children growing, learning and achieving, but, darn it, it breaks your heart to see them doing those things so fast! Allow these feelings to flow into your scrapbook pages by capturing the excitement for the kids and the welling pride from you.

Growing Independence

This page is about Amber's coming to terms with her son's increasing independence. "This is your last year of elementary school, but for me, this is a year of firsts," Amber writes in her journaling. Her son is too old to be walked to school by his mother, so that means no more photos with the teacher, photos in front of the school, etc. Instead, Amber caught glimpses of her pre-teen boy in the front yard and as he rode away on his bike. "It's a great picture to have," she says of the bike photo. "As a bonus, (your children) don't even know you're snapping that picture!"

SUPPLIES:
Patterned paper (Junkitz); chipboard accents (Basic Grey, Li'l Davis Designs); cardstock; acrylic paint; stamping ink; thread; circle punch; font (Steelfish)

Amber

Supplies

With three little girls, Heidi has definitely "been there, done that" when it comes to school shopping. This bright page oozes a carefree attitude, but the journaling shows Heidi's pragmatic side about buying school supplies. She recommends including prices of supplies—in the future, you'll be able to compare. She used fun back-to-school themed products, including pencil patterned paper and alphabet trim. She created the photo border by setting eyelets in a piece of rickrack and attaching padlock letter charms with clasps.

SUPPLIES:

Patterned paper (FMI, Plaid); clip board (Provo Craft); letter stamps (Lazar Studiowerx); charms (Around The Block); ribbon (Michaels); clasps, eyelets (Darice); cork (Magic Scraps); die-cut letters (Sizzix); stickers (Chatterbox); acrylic paint; fabric paper; fonts (DJ Groovy, Doodle Crayon)

Heidi

GETTING PHOTOS AT SCHOOL
Things you should know and photos you should get:

Always ask permission before shooting photos on the school grounds.

Be understanding of your child if he or she is anxious about your taking a lot of photos.

If you plan to submit for publication a scrapbook page that has images of lots of school children, get permission from the parents of the other kids.

If possible, photograph the classroom, your child's desk, your child's teacher, your child in front of the school and your child with his or her best friends.

Psst! In this chapter you will learn how to...

✳ manipulate line and shape in design

✳ create zesty titles

✳ use fonts for maximum effect

✳ catch some design rhythm

✳ work with big, bold patterns

✳ incorporate lots of photos into a layout

✳ find design inspiration from a photo

✳ use space efficiently on a layout

design

LIKE A PRO IN THE KNOW

Simple scrapbook-design solutions for flawless layouts

You have chosen your photos and written the journaling. You have bought the cutest papers and accents EVER. But yet you sit at your scrapbook workspace with a swelling sense of anxiety. Did you forget something? No. Is the journaling giving you fits? Not anymore. So, what gives?

Well, when it comes to layout design, something tells us you might prefer a few hours of manual long division to the challenge of conceptualizing fresh and exciting layout ideas. We feel your pain, but designing an ab-fab layout isn't that hard, you just need to brush up on a few tricks.

And, oh baby, do we have some tricks for you. After this chapter, your head will be spinning with ideas for your scrapbooks. Just sit back, clear the head and get ready to design some great pages.

My color choices are about as inspired as my husband on a Sunday afternoon. Show me three ways to take a color risk.

Color courage takes time and patience. But, you'll never earn it if you don't start experimenting. Start by noticing the color combinations in your everyday life. That billboard that you stare at while sitting in rush-hour traffic—do you dig the color combo? Try to incorporate it into a scrapbook page. Look at magazine ads and product packaging. Check out what mother nature has to offer. Make note of the inspiring combinations and try them in your scrapbooks.

merry & BRIGHT

Bright pink that is. I know red is the traditional color of Christmas, but Savannah thinks pink is perfect for any holiday. Pink pjs, pink Christmas ornaments, even a new pink Christmas sweater for Molly. What's next Savannah, a pink Halloween? How about a pink St. Patrick's Day? Savannah and Molly Dec. 2005

Vanessa

SUPPLIES:
Patterned paper (KI Memories); letter accents (Heidi Swapp); snowflake accents, rhinestones (EK Success); snowflake punch (Carl); cardstock; font (www.twopeasina bucket.com)

Buck Tradition

So, it's January, and you're hanging out in your scraproom, sighing over the holiday photos. You want to create unconventional pages, but a traditional red/green color combo is anything but exciting. What to do? Look to the photos for inspiration and go bold! Vanessa decided to let her daughter's totally chicky pj's dictate this color scheme. The pink/green combo is fresh, yet not too far off the mark for a holiday page.

Dust Off the Color Wheel

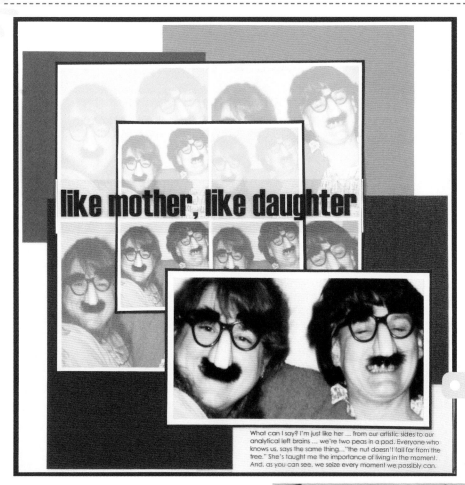

like mother, like daughter

What can I say? I'm just like her ... from our artistic sides to our analytical left brains ... we're two peas in a pod. Everyone who knows us, says the same thing... "the nut doesn't fall far from the tree." She's taught me the importance of living in the moment. And, as you can see, we seize every moment we possibly can.

It's small. It's round. It's colorful. It's necessary for taking real color risks. The color wheel will lead you into color universes that you never knew existed (FYI: planet tetrad is awesome!). Here, Torrey used the color wheel to develop a double split-complementary color scheme comprised of only tertiary colors (such as blue-green or yellow-green). It was a bold move, so she combined it with a Warhol-like effect: Using image-editing software, she colorized one image in four shades. She then grouped the shaded images together and printed.

SUPPLIES:
Textured cardstock (Prism); transparency; Photoshop Elements software

Torrey

PHOTOS: HEIDI FINGER

Go for Spice

Orange is an intimidating color for people to wear, let alone scrapbook with. Angie wanted a color scheme that conveyed her son's vibrant sense of humor. She chose to use orange as the background (she picked a slightly tangier hue than the orange of her son's shirt in the focal photo). The bold blue title creates a dynamic contrast. The green, a natural complement to blue, adds just a hint of verve to the scheme.

SUPPLIES:
Mini brads, letter brads (Queen & Co.); rub-ons (SEI); letter stickers (Chatterbox); colored pencils; notebook paper; cardstock

Angie

Excuse me, but all this mumbo jumbo about using line and shape in design eludes me. Explain it.

OK, try to look at this in basic terms: Every design, whether on a scrapbook page or within a piece of furniture, is constructed of lines and shapes. If you remove the patterns, colors and textures, you're left with a skeletal image of line and shape. The quality of the lines and shapes within your scrapbook page design should reflect the mood of your photos and journaling. If the photos are high energy, go for strong lines and bold shapes. If the photos are quiet, opt for gentle lines and delicate shapes. Easy.

SUPPLIES:
Patterned papers (Basic Grey); foam stamps, rub-ons (Heidi Swapp); chipboard (Grafix); pens; stamping ink; cardstock

Kelly

Guide the Eye

The lines and shapes in this layout shout with bold cuteness. Funky stars and exaggerated number shapes are playful. Kelly also employed the invisible lines of a visual triangle. Of course, the adorable photo draws our attention, but because Kelly centered this focal photo inside a visual triangle, our eyes stay there. The repeating "100" creates the points of the triangle.

Create Movement

In this layout, the ubiquitous dotted line becomes a function of form (rather than a function of a boring form letter). Amber loved the energy and movement inherent in the leaf patterned paper. She decided to mimic the dotted lines in the pattern with hand stitching and machine-sewed stitching details on the layered flower accents. These accents also help guide the eye around the page.

SUPPLIES:
Patterned paper (Chatterbox, Sassafras Lass); chipboard letters (Making Memories); buttons (Autumn Leaves); embroidery floss; stamping ink; font (www.autumnleaves.com)

When I saw this yellow wig in the Halloween clearance aisle—I knew that you would find great satisfaction in a "real" head of hair.

Bald as a baby, and your hair thin and fair now, you haven't quite been able to be the true princess you would like to be.

For a little while, you even placed a pair of pants on your head, the legs streaming down your back like the long mane you desired. It became a daily ritual. People passing by would just smile and they saw you shake your head from side to side, feeling your newfound locks sway from side to side.

But "real" hair is so much better! From the moment you first saw it you were certain it had to be yours. I obliged...and I can't help but smile every time I see you wear it.

Amber

Add Playfulness

This rambunctious layout benefits from several uses of line and shape. Julie began with number-patterned paper, which she felt supported a "keep life simple" theme. The pattern was playful, featuring an erratic design with bouncing circles. Julie echoed the circles throughout the rest of the design. Inspired by her son's striped shirt, she used strong horizontal lines in the form of orange strips of paper to help guide the eye to the photos.

Julie

SUPPLIES:
Patterned paper, paper tags (Basic Grey); chipboard letters, rub-ons (EK Success); brads, ribbon (Making Memories); cardstock

my boys

It's the simple things in life that make the world turn. Just to stop and take time from your busy day to give your daddy a hug and let me take a couple of pictures. Keep it simple and it will always be real.

just the two of us

fall 2004

daddy hayden

My titles are B-O-R-I-N-G. What are some ways to enliven them?

Titles can be a real terror. First, it's a pain in the butt to come up with a clever title, word-wise. Then, you're expected to do something cute and fancy with it, design-wise. Jeez! Word-wise, your title should be clear enough to tell the reader what your scrapbook page is all about. Design-wise, it should grab the reader and invite her to enjoy your scrapbook page. With all of the fonts, rub-ons, letter stickers, chipboard accents and more at our fingertips, terrific titles are easier than you think.

You are such a beautiful child. From the sparkle in your deep brown eyes to the perfect shape of your lips, your beauty is so mesmerizing. I just love this picture of you. You look so calm and angelic. And just for that split second, the silliness of your personality is not apparent. For just that exact moment, there was no sign of that teasing big sister that makes her little brother cry. No sign of the little girl who refuses to tidy up her room. The most particular drama queen is not anywhere to be found. With all the little things that make you YOU, you are just as beautiful on inside as you are on the outside. I love you.

Valerie S.

SUPPLIES:
Patterned papers (Basic Grey); rub-ons (Heidi Swapp, K & Company); chipboard accents (Heidi Swapp, Li'l Davis Designs, Pressed Petals); charms, rhinestones (K & Company)

Mix Media and Stack

Here's a recipe for a cool title, courtesy of Valerie: First, add a healthy helping of complementary patterns. Next, fold in some color. Add a dash of distressing. Now, divide the word and stack. This paper and chipboard title perfectly accents the charming photo of her daughter.

Think Outside the Box

Girl, if anyone ever tells you page titles always must be a certain way, shake that head and run! "Think beyond the square," Angelia says. For this page, a circle tag is the centerpiece from which the title radiates. The letters are hand cut, but you can achieve the same look with die-cut letters or alphabet stickers.

SUPPLIES:
Patterned paper, die-cut letters (My Mind's Eye); brads (Lasting Impressions); buttons (Autumn Leaves, Foofala); hinges (Boxer Scrapbook Productions); lace (source unknown)

Angelia

Add Dazzle

Holle is all about her titles. "Bold, bright titles are my signature touch on a layout," she says. For this title, she added pop and pizzazz with glitzy tinsel texture. Upper- and lowercase letters in different lettering styles add verve. She used foam adhesive, silk flowers and inked edges for dimension.

SUPPLIES:
Die-cut letters and animal shapes (QuicKutz); oval punch (Punch Bowl); flowers (Prima); brads (Creative Impressions); tinsel (Magic Scraps); cardstock; stamping ink

Holle

Expert Advice!

Use these title tips to draw the eye:

* Run a title vertically on a page for drama.

* Use a title to connect a two-page layout.

* Promote the page theme with the title via color, texture and style.

* Create an oversized title to help balance an oversized image on a single-photo layout.

* Compose a title from a variety of lettering styles and media to create movement.

Fonts are fun! How can I use them within my layout design for maximum effect?

Fonts are fun, and many scrapbookers are proud of their serious font collections. When designing with fonts, keep in mind a few simple guidelines. If you're going to mix fonts for an eclectic look, start the mix with three fonts and go from there—you want to entice with interest, not overwhelm with chaos. For journaling, make sure the font you use is readable. Feel free to spice it up by highlighting key words with funkier fonts. Don't forget to play with size and color. The best thing about working with fonts is your ability to customize!

Personalize Patterned Paper

Subtle, yes, but striking nonetheless. Vanessa added a little oomph to a vibrant faux-linen textured patterned paper by printing on it. For this sun-drenched page, she chose a carefree font and repeated the word "sun" so that it would cover an entire page (if you don't own a wide-format printer, simply trim a sheet of 12" x 12" paper to 8½" x 11"). Once printed, she used the paper as the center of her sun accent and as the backdrop to her journaling strips.

SUPPLIES:
Patterned paper (Basic Grey, My Mind's Eye); ribbon (American Crafts); rickrack (May Arts); chipboard accents (Heidi Swapp); brad, photo corners (Making Memories); stamping ink; thread; font (www.twopeasinabucket.com)

Vanessa

Think mood, contrast and readability when choosing a font | Journaling text should be printed in a readable font, while titles can be bold and full of energy. If you opt for a basic clean-lined font for the journaling, allow the title to contrast with something fun and flirty, if mood appropriate.

Print the font in an appropriate size | For journaling and other text blocks, experiment with point sizes 9 through 12. For titles, be sure the size is proportionate to the other page elements. The last thing you want is for the title to overpower the layout.

Fiddle with spacing | The space between the individual letters of a word or sentence is called kerning. Use it to tighten wide spaces or expand crowded letters. Kerning commands can normally be found under the Format menu in a word-processing program.

Supersize It

Bigger can definitely be better on a scrapbook page. On this page, Jessie penned her journaling on the computer and then altered the size of various lines of text. The graduating sizes of fonts helps draw attention to key ideas in her journaling.

SUPPLIES:
Patterned paper (Basic Grey, The Jennifer Collection); die cuts (Deluxe Designs); circle punch (Creative Memories); pen; font (Times New Roman)

Jessie

Capture Mood

And you thought you were moody. Fonts have more moods than any hormone-replacement therapy. For this page, Susan wanted to show a range of playfulness. She chose no less than seven fonts to describe her little poodle. To print the fonts so they appeared white, she created text boxes in a word processing document. She typed the words in an outline font into the boxes and selected the boxes with the cursor. She then added color to the boxes and removed color from the words with an outline function. She then printed on white cardstock.

SUPPLIES:
Patterned paper, ribbon (American Crafts); brads (Queen & Co.); thread; cardstock; fonts (www.scrapsupply.com, www.twopeasina bucket.com, Nilland, Eight Track, Century Gothic)

Susan W.

I know rhythm is an important design element. My pages aren't exactly shakin' their booties. Help!

We'd like you to repeat a phrase from Irene Cara's theme song from the movie *Flashdance* (1983), "I am rhythm now!" Yes, keep believin' because your pages are going to come alive! With fever! Rhythm is simple to achieve. All you need to do is repeat an element throughout your layout. Repeated elements can be an accent, a shape, color, texture, lines or photos. Always strive for balance and unity.

SUPPLIES:
Patterned paper, letter accents (Basic Grey); heart accent (Li'l Davis Designs); corner rounder; stamping ink; circle cutter; font (Arial Narrow)

Lisa V.

Repeat a Shape

Although it sounds odd to say that Lisa's lovely holiday page is bumpin', it's true. Her border of photos, all cropped to be the same-sized circle, creates a definite sense of rhythm. The photos all focus on a different detail of Christmas. She also rounded the corners of the page edges and journaling block for a sense of continuity.

Repeat an Accent

The repeating flower accent on this frame gives the design some twist and shout. Repetitive elements help keep a reader's eye moving around a design, but they also create a sense of unity in the piece. On this frame, the flowers definitely create rhythm, and the smaller accents of brads, rhinestones and ribbon leaves add to the effect. The continuous green stem also helps the eye stay on track.

SUPPLIES:
Patterned paper (Rusty Pickle); brads (Bazzill); die-cut flower (Sizzix); rhinestones (JewelCraft); ribbon (Offray); rickrack (Me & My Big Idea); paper wire (Paperbilities); glitter spray, stained glass paint (Krylon); stamping ink; decoupage medium; chipboard; foam adhesive

● **Denise**

Expert Advice!

More ways to give a page rhythm:

* Duplicate and reduce the focal photo and repeat the reduced image.

* Repeat a singular image, such as a sticker or die cut.

* Repeat a shape throughout the layout.

* Pick three colors to repeat throughout the layout.

Big patterns—they are bold and beautiful, but they're intimidating. How can I use them effectively?

Some grandmother once said to her granddaughter that it was distasteful to wear dresses with pattern motifs larger than a fist. Pish posh! Big patterns are in—big time. When you think about it, using large motif patterned paper can make page design easier. Obviously, the larger the element, the more space it's gonna need on a layout, so large motifs work well to balance an enlarged photo or strong title. Then, there's little room or need for further accents.

Looking at you in your daddy's arms at just five weeks old you look so small and delicate. So breakable. Every thing in my being just wants to protect you from the big, scary world. I don't think that feeling will ever go away no matter how old you get. God gave me this precious little girl to guide & watch over. If I could I would suffer every hurt for you & go through every trial in your place... but I can't. I can only shield you when I can, pray for you continuously & teach you how to weather the storms. You're so tiny now & life is simple. I know it won't always be so. I know this means little now as you are with me every moment, but I will always be here for you. You will always be my baby, Samantha.

Earth had swallowed all my hopes but she, She is the hopeful lady of my earth. -William Shakespeare

Little One

Sheila

SUPPLIES:
Patterned paper, paper flower (Chatterbox); label (Me & My Big Ideas); safety pin (Making Memories); flower rub-on (KI Memories); corner rounder; thread; image-editing software; fonts (Porcelain, PMingLiU)

Temper With Simpler Patterns

When it comes to pattern mixing, there can only be one star. Otherwise, the competition for attention gets nasty. For this girlie background, Sheila used papers from a coordinating line of patterned papers. She chose to balance the bold paisley design with smaller floral motifs. Sheila recommends this technique for single-photo layouts or those with black-and-white photos. "That way, the pattern isn't competing with a lot of color or action in the photos," she says.

Use Minimal Embellishment

A smart selection of paper is really all you need to create a stunning scrapbook page. Kathy layered less intense patterns over bolder prints for this background, which she embellished with only a pencil, ribbons and rub-ons. The papers came from a coordinating line of patterned papers, which ensured a spot-on color mix. Also when working with bold patterns, Kathy suggests throwing in some neutral colors. "The white mats and journaling block are neutrals that help balance the layout and separate the photos from the bright patterns," she says.

SUPPLIES:
Patterned paper (My Mind's Eye); rub-ons (EK Success, Making Memories); ribbon (American Crafts, Offray); stamping ink; pencil

Kathy

Cut Out Motifs

When we fall in love with a bold pattern, it's normally the repeated motif that we are drawn to as opposed to the entire sheet of paper. Armed with that knowledge, start looking at the parts of your bold patterns instead of the whole. Are there fun motifs that can be cut from the pattern and used on, say, a frame, like Suzy did here? Suzy cut the flowers from a sheet of paper and adhered them to a frame, which she first painted a neutral color. She then added a little glitz by adhering rhinestones to the flower centers.

SUPPLIES:
Patterned paper (Sandylion Sticker Designs); frame (source unknown); rhinestones (Darice, EK Success); acrylic paint; decoupage medium

Expert Advice!

More ways to subdue a bold pattern:

* Cover a bold pattern with vellum.
* Use a bold pattern to create photo mats and corners.
* Cut strips of paper from a bold patterned paper to use as a border.
* Distress a bold pattern with acrylic paint or sandpaper (or both!).

Suzy

PHOTO BY: TARA WHITNEY PHOTOGRAPHY

I love big, engaging images as much as the next gal, but sometimes I want to fit several photos onto a page. How can I do so gracefully?

Layouts with one super-enlarged and super-engaging focal image are elegant and captivating, but let's face facts, here. We're scrapbookers, so we're also avid, maybe even annoyingly relentless, photographers. The pictures are piling. When scrapbooking multiple photos on a layout, remember that there still must be a star photo. The other photos should play a supporting role. There are several ways to include this cast. Don't forget, you can always create a lightweight mini album full of photos that attaches to your page.

SUPPLIES:
Patterned paper (DieCuts with a View); chipboard accents (Heidi Swapp); letter stamps (Technique Tuesday); chipboard; stamping ink; pens; cardstock

Add a Group of Support Images

"My favorite way to fit multiple photos onto a page is by grouping same-sized support photos into one unit," Kelly says. By making this grouping a bit smaller than the focal photo, it does not compete for attention nor is detail sacrificed.

Use a Photo Border

Whether you need to show a series of events, action taking place or more detail, photo borders are an excellent option. Here, Amber picked the most compelling photo as the focal image and used the rest as support photos. With the photo border, Amber shows exactly how much fun her daughter is having playing in a pile of leaves. Each chosen photo shows a different expression of glee.

SUPPLIES:
Brads (Queen & Co.); leaf cutting template (Creative Memories); thread; chipboard; stamping ink; embroidery floss; cardstock; font (www.twopeasinabucket.com)

ALL THAT matters

You found this pile of leaves.
It kept you entertained for hours.
You came out a muddy mess.
A huge smile was glued to your face.
And that is all that matters.

2004

Amber

Create a Photo Montage

When it comes to fitting more photos on a page, remember two things, Christine says. First, keep the design fairly simple. Second, choose one or two key photos to enlarge for the focal point, leaving the rest to act as support images. For this layout, Christine essentially split her design in half. On the right side are the focal photos, on the left are the support photos (collected in a cool photo column) and journaling. "When determining which photos to place where, consider the lightness and color of each photo and try to put some distance between those of equal values," Christine says. "Your layout will have greater contrast and more appeal."

SUPPLIES:
Patterned paper (Basic Grey); chipboard accents (Heidi Swapp); brads (Making Memories); flower charm (Nunn Designs); corner punch (EK Success); stamps (Pixie Press); paper flowers (Prima); stamping ink; cardstock

Christine

I've been told to seek design inspiration from my photos. Exactly how do I do this?

Every inch of your scrapbook page should be inspired by the photos. The colors, the textures, the line and shape quality, the journaling, the title—everything. You simply need to study the photo and make note of elements to pull from it. The elements could come from clothing, the texture of the scenery, the sky, a person's eyes and facial features. Start by asking yourself, "What is the mood of the photo?" Then, pick colors, patterns, textures, and line and shape quality based on the mood.

Look for Patterns in Clothing

This should be a natural for most women since clothes are extremely high on our priority lists. When determining line direction and pattern for your layout, look at the clothes. Here, Danielle used the stripes on her son's shirt for inspiration. She mimicked the stripes by layering strips of cardstock for the background and also with striped ribbon.

SUPPLIES:
Brads, velvet ribbon (Making Memories); chipboard accents (Heidi Swapp); letter stamps (FontWerks); belt (Old Navy); vintage trim; brads; pen; cardstock

Danielle

"I created a glow-in-the-dark page. The paint, the thread and the polymer clay glow. Even the little fireflies twinkle on and off. I created a scrapbook page that is best viewed in total darkness!"
Torrey

Identify Textures

This page background acts as a perfect extension of these photos. When composing it, Angelia took cues from the photos—the gentle feel of spring discovery and the dainty eyelet dress her daughter is wearing. She first sought papers in colors synonymous with spring. The playful yet delicate prints and the soft greens, pinks and whites definitely support the spring theme. Then, Angelia added rickrack, ribbon, buttons and a rhinestone buckle to complete the page.

SUPPLIES:
Patterned papers (Scenic Route Paper Co.); flower punch (Family Treasures); letter stickers (American Crafts); buttons (Autumn Leaves, Foofala); rickrack, ribbon, rhinestone buckle (source unknown); transparency tab (Creative Imaginations); cardstock

I knew it from the time I first laid eyes on this dress. This dress said "MICHAELA" in big letters. Well, not really, but you know what I mean. Pink with white polka dots and green rick rack, with a frog, snail, and ladybug smocked across the front. What could be more perfect for your 6th birthday? Beautiful, happy, and playful. Sounds like "Michaela" to me, and you were tickled to wear it.

playful

Angelia

Repeat Line and Shape Quality

Lisa was moved by the repeating horizontal lines in this photograph. "The layers of the rocks, the line of the horizon and the horizontal lines of the clouds in the sky provided the inspiration to extend these lines from the actual borders of the photo," she says. "Extending these lines also helped create the feeling of vastness." To create her own layers of rock on the right side of the page, Lisa mixed acrylic paint with texture gels, which she applied to a recycled envelope. Once the paint dried on the envelope, Lisa melted the envelope with a heat gun to achieve the various textures and colors.

SUPPLIES:
Vellum (Grafix); texture gel (Liquitex); acrylic letters (KI Memories); acrylic paint; chalk; cardstock; font (Tahoma)

There is no photograph or documentary film or secondhand account that can prepare you for that first moment when you stand at the rim of the canyon and feast your eyes on the spectacular landscape spread before you. And while it's true your senses experience a great deal of its beauty, your spirit knows that its depth and breadth continue far beyond what the eyes can see and the senses feel – majestic and glorious.

September 21, 2005
Grand Canyon National Park

canyon

Lisa D.

Must I fill the entire layout with elements? Must I leave space on my layout?

Scrapbook page design can turn you into a space case if you let it. But, really, there is no right or wrong way to handle the white space on a layout. Layouts with zero white space exude energy and movement. If that's what the photos and memory demand, go for it with gusto. If photos and sentiments are more relaxed or contemplative, creating a clean layout with large expanses of open space is certainly a solid and classic design choice.

This couple is my example in life. They showed me how to love. They showed me how to laugh. They showed me how to serve. They showed me how to live life to the fullest. They showed me how to be a good partner. They showed me how to be a good parent. And most important, they showed me how to be an example myself.

Amber

SUPPLIES:
Patterned paper (My Mind's Eye); transparency; chipboard letters (Making Memories); thread; cardstock; font (www.autumnleaves.com)

Create Drama With Space

Having few photos of her parents, Amber cherishes this image. She wanted to give it complete attention, so by bathing the enlarged and closely-cropped image in white, she achieves the goal. "This clean layout shows you can have good white space and still have a feminine romantic design," Amber says. She used the "rule of thirds," thereby ensuring an interesting and balanced layout. The flower accents were hand cut from patterned paper with a craft knife. Amber sanded the edges to further distress them.

Infuse With Energy

This wild, filled-to-the-rim layout design is just as vibrant as its photos. To show the busyness of a parade, Susan chose strong primary and bright colors and a mix of textures. She also combined strong straight lines with dancing polka dots and wavy rickrack. The strong lines keep the eye moving through the layout, from start to finish.

SUPPLIES:
Patterned paper (Karen Foster Design); rickrack (Me & My Big Ideas); ribbon, bookplate (unknown source); buttons (Doodlebug); embroidery floss; brads (Making Memories); typewriter key (EK Success); cardstock; font (www.twopeasinabucket.com)

Susan C.

DESIGN WITH THE RULE OF THIRDS
This concept divides space within equal thirds.

The thirds are created by a grid of intersecting horizontal and vertical lines. In layout design, divide your background into thirds (columns or rows) and place page elements on intersections.

When designing a layout, avoid placing "elements of interest" dead center. Otherwise, you risk creating a boring layout. The focal point should fall on one of the intersections. If working with an enlarged portrait, place facial features, such as the eyes or mouth on the intersections.

This layout is an excellent example of using the "rule of thirds." Dividing the layout into three columns, you can see that Susan placed the subject of the photo at an intersection. The divisions between the photo, title block and journaling block also show great use of this rule.

Psst! In this chapter you will learn how to...

✳ include stitching on your layouts

✳ make contemporary paper piecings

✳ use the benefits of digital scrapbooking

✳ distress with grace and ease

✳ execute edgy edge effects

✳ build interactive page elements

✳ add pizzazz to color blocking

✳ combine patterns

✳ use only paper, pens and photos to create a layout

✳ incorporate your child's artwork into your scrapbook

✳ display scrapbook art in your home

learn

THE SKILLS TO CREATE SCRAPBOOK THRILLS

The techniques, the tips and the tricks to create great looks and hot styles

We know you began scrapbooking for the higher purpose of preserving your family's memories and histories for generations to come. You love the hobby because, through your scrapbook pages, your family can see your immense love for them.

Indeed. But, might there be another reason for loving this hobby? Face it, you're also in it for the accolades. The oohs. The ahhs. The "how'd you do that?" exclamations from friends and relatives who remain bedeviled by your creative genius.

Shameless as it sounds, we just love that part about scrapbooking, too. So, in this chapter, we're going to dish out our best tips, tricks and techniques that are guaranteed to result in jaw-dropping, drool-inducing, tear-jerking pages.

What are three easy ways to include stitching on my layout?

Itchin' for some stitchin' on your pages? We're glad to hear it because it's an easy way to add texture and a finishing touch to layouts. If you have a sewing machine, start experimenting on scrap paper. Play with the stitching functions, thread color or embroidery abilities, if your machine has the skills. For hand stitching, grab a wide-eyed needle, a paper piercer and some embroidery floss (it's thicker than thread). Pierce the paper in your desired pattern before you stitch for best results.

SUPPLIES:
Patterned paper (SEI);
plastic letters (Heidi Swapp);
rub-on letters (American
Crafts); stamp (Leave Memories);
flower accents (Queen & Co.);
stamping ink; floss; cardstock;
font (Avant Garde)

Lisa V.

Stamp and Stitch

If you've never stitched on a page before, this is a technique with a low fear factor. On the right side of the layout is a bouquet of paper flowers with stitched stems. Lisa used a flower stamp to create the stems (she cut off the stamped petals). She cut them out and then detailed them with an easy straight stitch (use a paper piercer to punch stitching holes). She finished the flowers with shiny paper flower accents.

Subtle Trims

Since creating this layout, Diana has changed her tune in regard to stitching. "I always swore that I would not sew on pages," she says emphatically. "Sewing and I do not mix well." But, after seeing the ease of adding soft sewing accents, Diana does not stress over sewing. When used as an accent and not the featured technique, sewing is fun, she says. "And, if you are after a rustic feel for your page, it doesn't matter if the sewing is crooked!"

SUPPLIES:
Patterned paper, sticker border, tab, frame (My Mind's Eye); rub-on letters (Making Memories); rub-on flower, photo corner (Heidi Swapp); rub-on word (7 Gypsies)

Diana G.

Embroidered Swirls

Swirly stitches add lots of girly fun to scrapbook pages. Valerie hand stitched swirls to create a delicate feminine border for this page that celebrates her mother's joy at being a grandmother. The soft curves of the stitched accents mimic the beautiful organic shapes found in the patterned paper.

SUPPLIES:
Patterned papers (We R Memory Keepers); letter accents (EK Success); ribbon (Offray); rhinestones (K & Company); embroidery floss

Valerie S.

I love watching my mom interact with her grandchildren. She adores her two granddaughters, that is for certain. Because Grandma Pia & Ashley live in California, Lauren only sees them about twice a year. We enjoyed spending time with them during their last visit in Thanksgiving 2005. As usual, Grandma Pia doted and spoiled them with gifts and attention, which they enjoyed. We cannot wait until the next time we see them again. We all miss them so very much!
Nov. '05. Lauren (5), Ashley (10)

Paper piecing seems, you know, so five minutes ago. But I like it. How can I create my own contemporary designs?

Just because paper piecing is a little dated doesn't mean it can't be resurrected with en vogue techniques. Basically, we've outgrown the cutesy bear and bunny patterns (not that they don't have a place on baby pages or those created about young children). Now, we're much more into chic fashionista designs, ultra cool flower motifs and anything with an avant-garde look to it. Put on your imagination cap, grab your pencils, paper and craft knife and get ready for some paper piecing of mind.

Mimic the Light and Shadow of a Photograph

Caution: Proceed with patience! This artwork is beautiful, but its re-creation requires meticulous attention to detail, a steady hand and an ample supply of sharp craft knife blades. A silkscreen print inspired this technique, Torrey says. Using image-editing software, she altered a photo of Jodi so the color values would be more pronounced. She chose papers to match the values and determined how those colors would be layered. Next, she printed several images of the altered photo on regular paper. From the printed photos, she cut out each individual color value and temporarily adhered them to the corresponding cardstock. She cut the shapes from the cardstock, removed the templates and any adhesive, ran the cardstock pieces through an adhesive-application machine and immediately adhered to the paper piecing.

SUPPLIES:
Textured cardstock (Prism); photo turns; brads; transparency; image-editing software; adhesive-application machine (Xyron); craft knife

Torrey

Seek Inspiration From Ads

Want fresh paper-piecing ideas? "Just look around you," begs Vanessa. She finds inspiration for paper piecing (and her scrapbooking, in general) EVERYWHERE! These funky feminine flower designs were inspired by a motif she saw in a Pottery Barn catalog. She traced the flower designs freehand onto white textured cardstock. After cutting out the leaves and stems, she swabbed each with acrylic paint in springy colors. Once dry, she added pen details, adhered the flower centers with foam adhesive and finished with cute little tags that she attached with string and black hooks.

SUPPLIES:
Tags, flowers (Sizzix); buttons (Making Memories); clip (Heidi Swapp); hook (Prym-Dritz); pen; cardstock; font (www.twopeasinabucket.com)

Vanessa

Use Clip Art

Some scrapbookers hiss at the mere mention of the phrase "clip art." It can conjure images that today's modern scrapbooker shudders at. But, trust us, clip art can be cool. In fact, that swank flourish gracing the cover of this album hails from clip art. Jessica reverse-printed the clip art image onto the back of patterned paper (three different pieces) and cut it out. She layered the pieces for a funky effect.

SUPPLIES:
Patterned paper (Basic Grey); album (American Crafts); clip art (www.doverpublications.com); chipboard letters (Heidi Swapp); cardstock

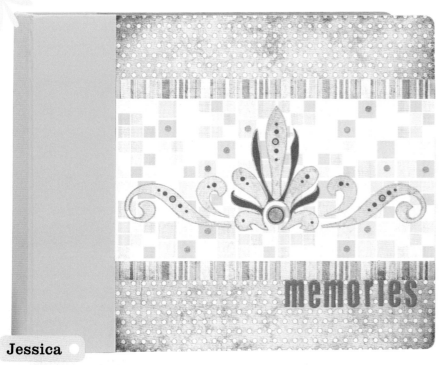

Jessica

Expert Advice!

How to create an original pattern:

1. Find a photo or image of the object from which you wish to base the paper piecing.

2. Scan the image. Before scanning, select the desired proportion size. For example, if the image you are scanning is smaller than the paper piecing you wish to create, be sure to scan the image at an enlarged size. Print the image.

3. Cover the printed image with white paper and trace the individual parts of the image onto the paper. (Use a lightbox if possible.)

4. Cut out the pieces and trace the shapes on various colors of cardstock. Cut those out and piece them together.

A lot of scrapbookers are raving about digital scrapbooking. What are the benefits I should consider?

You can't deny the convenience of technology. Yes, sometimes we have the urge to throw out the cell phones or perform percussive maintenance on the computer, but the fact is that digital stuff makes tasks quicker and easier. The same goes for digital scrapbooking. Pages can be created more quickly and less expensively. They can be shared and duplicated. Creative control is total, which is a major plus.

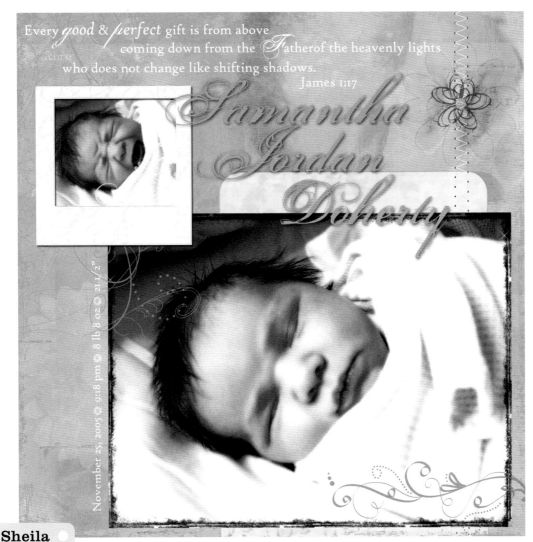

SUPPLIES:
Digital background and accents (Autumn Leaves, www.shabbyprincess.com); image-editing software

Sheila

Easy to Share

After the birth of her daughter and fourth (yes, fourth!) child, Sheila created a digital scrapbook page that also served as a birth announcement. Each family member was able to print a high-quality image of the page. "To create the same layout with paper several times and mail it, or to scan and e-mail a paper layout, would be much more difficult and the quality would not be as high," Sheila says.

Easy to Do

Drag and drop. Digital scrapbooking is that easy. Moreover, Susan notes, digital scrapbooking is less expensive: "You can load up your page with multiples of the same element for the same price as using one." For this page, Susan purchased a digital chipboard alphabet set, which she resized and recolored to create the eclectic title. She still owns the original digital files of the alphabet to use on hundreds of layouts to come.

SUPPLIES:
Digital background and accents (www.heatheranndesigns.com, www.digitaldesignessentials.com, digitalscrapbookmemories. com); image-editing software

Susan C.

No Clean Up

Just think of the mess Jessica would have made had she created this layout from paper. Instead, this digital layout, which looks remarkably lifelike, was mess-free and easy to create. Jessica used a swirl brush tool to stamp the waves that float from her daughter's face. "These curves help break up the blocky page design and would be very difficult to create in a paper layout," Jessica says.

SUPPLIES:
Digital papers, digital overlay (www.designerdigitals.com); digital brush (Autumn Leaves); image-editing software

Jessica

Distressing is way cool.
What are some funky, fresh ideas?

As women, we fret with each and every wrinkle (are our faces really losing value?), but a scrapbook layout with wrinkled paper, well, it looks downright distinguished! It's ironic how distressing techniques are so stylish that layouts without them risk being labeled as outdated. A little sandpaper and brown and black ink will go a long way toward making layouts super fabulous.

Kelly

SUPPLIES:
Patterned papers (Cherry Arte, K & Company, Provo Craft); chipboard accents (Heidi Swapp); rub-ons (Doodlebug Design); 3-D sticker (Provo Craft); stamping ink; pen; cardstock

Inked Layers

Look at Kelly, trying to trick our eyes! Her inking technique gives the journaling strips and photo the appearance of mats. First, she inked the edges of each element with bright yellow. Once dry, she went over the yellow with charcoal. The contrast gives the illusion of depth.

Sandpaper

Suzy loves using sandpaper as a part of her distressing routine. "I like to spritz paper lightly with water, crumple it, iron it, sand it, sew around the edges and tear and fray the edges," she says. That's precisely what she did on this layout to create the flower accent in the top left corner. She also distressed a piece of white paper, which she used to cover the chipboard letters.

SUPPLIES:
Patterned paper (Bo-Bunny Press, Creative Imaginations, Déjà Views); chipboard accents (Heidi Swapp); buttons (source unknown); embroidery floss; pen; thread

Suzy

PHOTO: TARA WHITNEY PHOTOGRAPHY

Liquids and Powders

Distressing works great with heritage pages. Here Denise combined basic distressing with heat embossing on her journaling, creating a faux-tile appearance. She started by sponging a small envelope with cream acrylic paint and then inking the edges with brown. To print on it, she taped it to a piece of paper and ran it through the printer. Then she applied double-sided tape to the front and sprinkled with clear embossing powder. After heating the powder, the envelope was left with a highly textured surface.

SUPPLIES:
Patterned paper (Basic Grey, Daisy D's, Rusty Pickle); envelope (Columbian); lace (Offray, Wrights); ribbon (Stampendous); brads (Making Memories); photo corners (The Eggery Place); bookplate, watch face (EK Success); alphabet charms (The Paper Studio); string; gold leaf; stamping ink; acrylic paint; embossing powder; foam adhesive

Denise

I love edge effects!
What are three creative effects?

Like the perfect scarf or those earrings that add spark to any outfit, edge effects are the ultimate finishing touch to a page. Subtle yet attention-getting, they invite readers to "ooh" and "ahh" over your artwork. And, because every page element has an edge of some sort, the creative possibilities are limitless. Edge effects can be created by sanding elements or inking techniques. Oh, and remember all those decorative-edge scissors you bought five years ago? How about dusting those off?

I am saddened and angry with myself.

In the two years since Quinn's birth, these are the only photos that I have of my 4 children together.

How could I let all this time pass without gathering them for a family photo? How come the idea to take a group shot hasn't occurred to me more? Why do I keep putting off a picture that I know I will cherish?

I love seeing my children together. I love seeing the older boy's arms secured around their younger siblings. I adore the expressions of pride and happiness that the little ones exude towards their older brothers.

No more waiting! Today, I will take the kids out, set them down together, and make this a priority. I will mark on my calendar a day each month to take 5 minutes out of our day to take some pictures.

Amber

SUPPLIES:
Patterned paper (Chatterbox); chipboard accents (Basic Grey); button (Autumn Leaves); acrylic paint; thread; cardstock; font (www.autumnleaves.com)

Scalloped Edges

The blue scalloped edge of the photo and journaling block is as spunky as it is sweet. Amber created it with the help of her sewing machine. First, she applied iron-on fusible fabric to the blue paper to stabilize it. She then placed it on the floral background paper. She ran it through her sewing machine to create the scallop edge and tore the excess from the top and bottom. She finished by adding the framed photo and journaling.

Nitty-Gritty Edges

Had it not been for the inky edges of these paper blocks, this layout would appear flat and dull. Instead, the page is ripe with texture and depth. Sharon inked textured cardstock with a dark, rich ink and chalk, creating a look of ink that is bleeding into the photo mats and blocks. The accentuated frames help guide the eye around the layout.

SUPPLIES:
Stamping ink; chalk; mesh; cardstock

Sharon

A BOY

HIS DAD

A LESSON LEARNED

THE MAN

Destination

windows to the past
Over the years, Paul has found much money laying on the ground. From pennies to bills, once even $70. While our daughters and I walk right by, and never take notice, he has spotted it and scoops it up and puts it in his pocket. Once, it was a $20 bill that the three of us walked over, but not him. He has heeded his dad's advice since he was just a boy. Reward comes to all who remember the lesson. He never seemed to trip much either.

Lesson # 1
Dad says, " Keep your head down so you don't trip over your feet. What you lookin' up for? Money don't fall up!"

Shabby Chic Edges

This shabby chic inspired frame is completely chic and anything but shabby. Angelia began with a premade frame. She sanded the outside edges as well as the edges of the photo window. Next, she scuffed them by running the blade of her scissors across the edges. To finish, she applied bright pink paint to the edges with a foam brush. Once dry, she did one final sanding job.

SUPPLIES:
Frame, silk flower, bookplate (Heidi Swapp); paper flower, tag (Making Memories); stickers (EK Success, Imagination Project); stencil (Autumn Leaves); epoxy accents (Provo Craft); acrylic paint; ribbon; rickrack; button

Angelia

time flies

Sweet

V

treasure

valuable: adj. Havi
sirable or esteemed char
istics or qualities. 2.Wo
good price. [FRIENDSHIP]

LAUGH

I LOVE YOU

"I'm a big fan of the curled edge. I sew close to the edge of a layer or element. I then dip my fingers in a tiny bit of water and just roll the edges. I love the dimension this adds." **Nic**

Interactive pages are neato! What are some EASY ways to create interactive elements?

Interactive pages are pretty sweet. They invite curious onlookers to come and play. Those who accept the standing invitation are thrilled to find hidden photos and journaling or other interesting elements that are the brain child of ingenious scrapbookers. While creating moving elements seems tricky, usually they are made functional by simple hinges or book-binding tape.

Danielle

SUPPLIES:
Patterned paper (Bo-Bunny Press, Creative Imaginations, K & Company, Provo Craft); decorative tape (Heidi Swapp); buttons (Autumn Leaves, Bazzill, Wal-Mart); chipboard accents (Maya Road); gaffer tape (7 Gypsies); embroidery floss; alphabet stickers (Making Memories); metal alphabet (American Crafts) pen; permanent marker; stamping ink

Journaling Tabs

For this "Q & A" style layout, Danielle thought flip-up journaling strips would add playfulness and intrigue. She lined the bottom of the layout with three journaling strips and attached them with buttons. On the front she posed questions to her son, asking him about his favorite toy, food and word. On the back of the strips lie the answers.

Torrey's Fashion Filosophy

When the word came down that Memory Makers was moving their operations to Cincinnati...I decided to look at the bright side. So every day, I went into Memory Makers and shaped my Fashion Filosophy...to help keep spirits up...

Attach Filosophy Here

You can dress her up... but you can't take her anywhere

SUPPLIES: Patterned paper (Me & My Big Ideas); magnet paper (Avery); spiral clips (Creative Impressions); clipboard clip (Design Originals); lettering template (Pagerz); pen; hole punch; image-editing software; foam core; rhinestones; cardstock

Torrey

PHOTOS: ROBERT "SCOTTY" SCOTT

Paper Dolls

Some people create interactive pages that ask readers to pull out journaling cards or flip through a book of pictures. Torrey allows people to play dress-up with a paper doll created in her image. This page of "fashion filosophies" is complete with a mini paper Torrey (created with the help of image-editing software) and several custom outfits, which were crafted on textured cardstock and adhered to magnetic paper. Each outfit comes complete with a philosophy that can be removed and added to the little orange clipboard.

Color blocking is such a great and easy technique, but it's so...blocky. How can I give it some pizzazz?

Pizzazz comes in many, many forms, especially in regard to color blocking. Spicing up a color-blocked background can be as simple as adding a block or two of patterned paper. You can also add stitching or sift through your stash of leftover stickers, rub-ons and other doodads to see if there's anything worthy to add (we'll bet you ten bucks that there is!).

"Rowen, show me your trains."

As far as you're concerned, the best game in the world is playing with your trains in the windowsill of the dining room. You line them up, you hook them together, you make train noises, and generally lose yourself in the moment. So when I said, "Rowen, show me your trains," I expected to be ignored. Instead, you took your two favorites out of the line and held them up next to your face for me to see. My heart just about breaks for the sweetness of this moment. Thank you, sweet girl, for being a big fan of trains and their sounds. Thank you for looking over once in a while when I ask you to show me something. And thank you for simply being you, every day. I love you, my sweet girl. 03.06

(Thanks.)

Jessica

SUPPLIES:
Patterned paper (Basic Grey, Chatterbox); chipboard accents (Basic Grey, Heidi Swapp); paper flower (Chatterbox); cardstock; font (www.twopeasina bucket.com)

Get Curvy

Real women know how to use their curves. Jessica proves this point with a super fresh approach to color blocking. The curving lines of the blocks add a real sense of movement to the page. To begin, Jessica drew a pattern guide for a conventional blocked background, minus the curves. Then, to add the curves, she used a large round plate to trace curving lines over the straight blocked background. She then cut out the new curvy blocks and used them as patterns to cut her papers, which she reassembled on her background of brown cardstock.

Add Patterns and Accents

Stripes, numbers, dotted lines, the alphabet—Angelia left no pattern unturned for her color blocking piece. She began with a layered background of red and white papers, then built upon the white with a colorful landscape of patterns. Next, she enhanced her vibrant layout with stitches, buttons and brads. Chipboard letters create a simple yet impactful title perched above her striking focal photo.

SUPPLIES:

Patterned paper (KI Memories, Scrapworks); decorative tape, chipboard accent, ghost letters (Heidi Swapp); brad (Making Memories); corner rounder (EK Success); buttons; staples; cardstock

Angelia

Cut Shapes Into the Blocks

Simple curves cut into this blocked background really add the pow and the wow to this layout. "I love color blocking," Jodi says, "but sometimes it needs something more." Jodi was trying to figure out how to include the "bubble" theme in her design. It dawned on her to add some bubbles to the background. She assembled the page background, minus the pink paper, onto a cutting mat. She then used a circle cutter to cut out the circle shapes. Finally, she reassembled the blocks on top of the pink cardstock.

SUPPLIES:

Patterned paper (Bo-Bunny Press); acrylic alphabet (Heidi Swapp, Karen Foster Design); staples (Making Memories); transparency; circle cutter; cardstock

Jodi A.

Expert Advice!

Ideas for putting the color in color blocking.

* Mix a bold color with neutrals for subtle color drama.

* Add energy to a page with a split-complementary or tetrad color combination (enlist the help of a color wheel to choose colors).

* Add patterned paper into the mix.

* Pair complementary colors for lots of zing.

What are some fun ways to combine patterned papers to create a custom background?

The fine art of mixing patterns requires a deft hand. Follow these simple guidelines for mixing patterns and you'll have the deftest hand at your crop table. Start with a mix of three patterns. As you become more confident, try mixing more, but be careful not to mix a confusing mess of motifs. All of the papers should have the same base color—for example, don't mix white-based papers with cream-based papers or the mix will look muddied. Look for patterns that have a variety of scale—don't use only patterns with small motifs or patterns with large motifs.

Suzy

SUPPLIES:
Patterned paper (Anna Griffin, Autumn Leaves, Bo-Bunny Press, Creative Imaginations, NRN Designs); plastic letters (Heidi Swapp); felt, buttons (source unknown) embroidery floss; pen

Kaliedoscope

This technique is easier than you think. The background is basically a series of squares of graduating sizes. Each square is comprised of four triangles of patterned papers. To begin, pick about a dozen patterned papers. For the first layer, quarter four sheets of the paper into triangles of equal size. Reassemble a square using a triangle from each pattern. Repeat these steps to create two more squares of smaller sizes.

Complementary Stripes

When creating a background, you're often told to mix organic shapes, such as flowers, with geometric shapes, such as squares. That is excellent advice, but sometimes layering similar patterns creates just as much drama. The trick, though, is to pick patterns in contrasting colors. For this beachcomber page, Nic layered blue striped paper on top of orange striped paper. The recurring stripes add movement and unity while the color contrast adds pop.

SUPPLIES:
Patterned paper (3 Bugs in a Rug); chipboard letters (Chipboard Chatter, Pressed Petals); chipboard accents (Maya Road); acrylic paint; rhinestones (Making Memories); ribbon (Strano Designs); cardstock; fonts (Century Gothic, www.twopeasinabucket.com)

Nic

Curvy Shapes

This layout throws a curve at the notion that pattern paper mixes need to be made up of blocks. Using a circle cutter, Valerie cut sheets from a coordinating set of patterned papers into circles and wavy strips. The result is a gentle and feminine background apropos for this mother-daughter portrait.

SUPPLIES:
Patterned papers, paper flowers (Heidi Grace); chipboard letters (Pressed Petals); rickrack (Wrights); circle cutter (Sizzix); cutting system for curved lines (Creative Memories); ribbon (Michaels); font (Prissy Frat Boy)

Valerie S.

PHOTO: JODI BRATCH

I'm a bit of a minimalist when it comes to scrapbooking. What are some ideas for cool scrapbook pages that use only paper, photos and pens?

If you are plagued by creative block, lack of time or running low on supplies (and money!), simplify! Getting back to the real basics of scrapbooking is an awesome creative challenge. Think of all the paper-crafting techniques you can use, such as color blocking, tearing and pattern mixing. With pens, you can fill your pages with doodles and journaling. And the photos, of course, are going to take center stage on layouts such as these.

bedtime routine

Our nightly ritual - a few bedtime stories and prayer, followed by butterfly kisses and nose rubs from Mommy and Daddy. Sweet dreams, son! 3/14/04

SUPPLIES:
Patterned papers (Autumn Leaves, Chatterbox); cardstock; pen

Joanna

Layered Papers and Scribble Frames

"Minimal supplies does not necessarily mean minimalist designs," Joanna declares. This page is definitely proof of that. On the layout, Joanna uses several tricks that make the most out of a small pool of supplies. First, she chose to work with energetic patterned papers. Next, the layered look of the layout—overlapping photos and the appearance of several layers of background paper—add dimension. Pen work also adds zip to the layout—Joanna used a white pen to draw funky frames and doodles on the photo mats and journaling blocks. Torn paper edges and the use of a digital photo filter provide the finishing touches.

Susan W.

Funky Journaling Border

Yes, this page would be so easy to re-create if only your handwriting were as nice as Susan's. Chin up, that's what lettering templates are for, or instead of handwritten journaling, create a text border on your computer. Susan was inspired by her best friend's spunky personality for this page, so she chose upbeat, bright papers.

SUPPLIES:
Patterned paper (SEI); cardstock; pen; stamping ink

Patterned-Paper Accents

Lisa used minimal supplies for maximum effect on this page. (Lisa has a deft hand when it comes to wielding a craft knife. Try less detailed patterns if you are not comfortable making fine cuts.) Using a craft knife, she cut flowers from a set of coordinating patterned papers. She sprinkled the flowers on her page background and then traced around them with a white pen.

SUPPLIES:
Patterned paper (Paper Loft); cardstock; pen; circle punch

Lisa V.

Expert Advice!

More ideas for scrapbooking with only a few supplies:

* Punch simple geometric shapes, such as circles and squares, from paper and use to create a background, border or photo mat.

* Create custom background paper by layering words typed in different fonts and font sizes.

* Use stamping ink to create colorwashed photo mats and journaling blocks.

How can I use my scrapbooking skills to preserve/display my child's artwork?

Little artists (your kids) value the praise of big artists (you) more than anything. Imagine how excited your little Picasso will be when he sees his own masterpieces prominently displayed in your scrapbooks. Incorporating your child's artwork into your own will not only encourage him to continue to explore his creativity, it will also infuse your own with pride and inspiration.

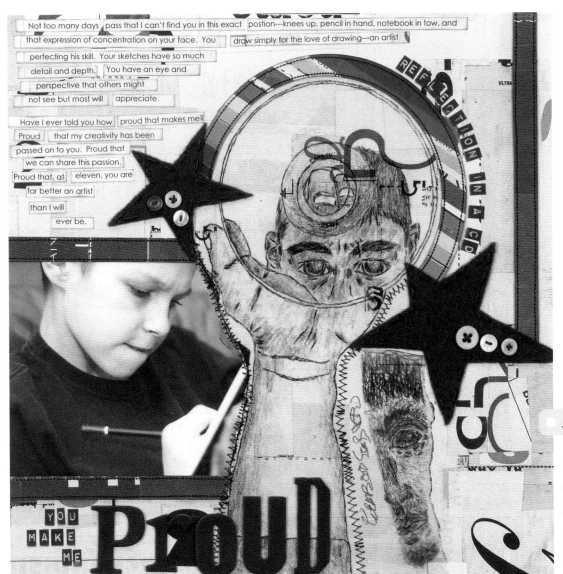

Not too many days pass that I can't find you in this exact postion---knees up, pencil in hand, notebook in tow, and that expression of concentration on your face. You draw simply for the love of drawing---an artist perfecting his skill. Your sketches have so much detail and depth. You have an eye and perspective that others might not see but most will appreciate.

Have I ever told you how proud that makes me? Proud that my creativity has been passed on to you. Proud that we can share this passion. Proud that, at eleven, you are far better an artist than I will ever be.

Amber

SUPPLIES:
Patterned paper, letter stickers (K & Company); chipboard letters (Heidi Swapp); transparency; acrylic paint; stamping ink; buttons; felt; fusible web; embroidery floss; font (Century Gothic)

Print on a Transparency

Like mother, like son. It's pretty obvious to see where this boy gets his creative spirit—from his mother. Amber wanted everything about this layout to showcase her son's ability. From the patterned papers to the broken-caption journaling style, the page is graphic and edgy. The masterpiece touch comes in the form of the custommade transparency. Amber scanned her son's drawing and printed it onto a self-adhesive transparency. Amber tore and inked the edges of the transparency because the original drawing was created on torn paper.

Scan and Reduce

These mini masterpieces were created from scanned and reduced artwork. Suzy loves that her daughter Sophie loves to create as much as she does. Here, Suzy picked three of her favorite pieces, scanned and reduced them, printed them on archival paper and highlighted them with premade frames.

SUPPLIES:
Patterned paper (Bo-Bunny Press); textured paper (FiberMark); rub-ons (Doodlebug Design, Making Memories); brads (Making Memories, Queen & Co.); trim; pen

Suzy

Create an Extra Special Frame

This shadowbox frame is art-gallery caliber with an added touch of funk. When Jessie found this frame at her local craft store, her eyes grew to masterpiece proportions. She removed the glass and added a cork backing (making it easy to pin up the latest designs from Miss Violet, her daughter). She then decorated the frame with bits of patterned paper, funky flower die cuts and her daughter's name (stamped).

SUPPLIES:
16 x 20" shadowbox frame (Michaels); patterned paper (KI Memories); letter stamps (Technique Tuesday); die-cut flowers (Deluxe Designs); paper flowers (Prima); cork tiles; stamping ink

Jessie

I would love to display my scrapbook art in my home. What are some creative ways to do it?

The next time you rearrange the living room or redecorate, instead of pining for a beautiful masterpiece by another artist, create your own. Scrapbooking has transcended the album by showing up on family room walls everywhere. Projects can be as simple as small accent frames or as grandiose as a group of four 16" x 16" canvas scrapbook pages.

Valerie S.

SUPPLIES:
Patterned papers, flower accents, shadowbox frame, letter stickers, rhinestones, plastic tag (K & Company); ribbon, rickrack, trim (Making Memories); wooden monogram (source unknown); cardstock

Build a Shadow Box

When you use a shadow-box frame to house scrapbook art, you can go crazy with dimension. "Actually, the artwork looks better with a great deal of dimension," Valerie says. For this page, which she created for her daughter's room, she gave several accents depth with foam adhesive.

Sass Up Storage Supplies

As if your scraproom were not enough of a testament to your creative prowess, rub it in everyone's face by dolling up your storage supplies. As Vanessa can attest, this pretty crate/bottle set not only serves as storage, it provides creative inspiration as well. "The fun papers and cute tags make me want to open a bottle and start scrapping," she beams. To decorate, she simply added strips of patterned paper to the crate and circles of patterned paper to the bottle tops. She finished with fun polka-dot ribbon on the crate and bottles and added tags to the bottles.

SUPPLIES:
Patterned paper (Junkitz); ribbon (American Crafts, May Arts); crate and bottles (Prima); tags (QuicKutz); buttons; pen; cardstock

Vanessa

Frame It

With each season comes a new opportunity to display scrapbook art, Angie says. At home, she has a book easel that rests on a table behind her sofa. Each season, she creates a family portrait scrapbook page, frames it and sets it on the easel. She suggests also placing the frame on a mantel or using ribbon to hang it on a wall.

SUPPLIES:
Patterned papers (Bo-Bunny Press, Daisy D's); flowers (Prima); tag (Déjà Views); rub-ons (Memories Complete); brads (Bazzill, Making Memories); ribbon (Xyron); frame; cardstock

Angie

Expert Advice!

More ideas for displaying scrapbook art in your home:

* Use stretched canvas (available in the traditional 12" x 12" size as well as a variety of larger and smaller sizes) as a background for scrapbook wall art.

* Print calendar sheets from a word processing program and create a custom calendar. Embellish with stickers and other favorite supplies.

* Design a chore board that is fun and creative.

* Embellish unpainted photo frames to display family portraits or school photos.

Psst! In this chapter you will learn how to...

* use leftover supplies
* include fabric on your layouts
* create cool ribbon accents
* use cutting templates in new ways
* get creative with found objects
* get excited about extra brads and eyelets
* freshen up stickers and die cuts
* mix alphabet stamp styles

* fall in love with pens and markers again
* take the shadow stamp to the next level
* get the most from a set of basic punches

accents

Fresh ways to use old favorites

Do you ever gaze at your scrapbook workspace with the same apathy normally reserved for your clothes closet, hours before a big night out? You know, that "but I have nothing to wear!" look that sends your husband fuming to his armchair purgatory.

Just like the closet in your bedroom, your scrapbook workspace no doubt is full of items you've grown tired of or simply forgotten about. It's probably a safe bet that some items have never been used!

Well, it's time to give the lame some game. Before you head out to buy even more tools and supplies that will eventually collect dust, learn how to use what you've got in fresh and exciting ways. Here, we will show you wonderful uses for leftover products and new ways to use old supplies. Soon, you'll lovingly remember why you bought all these fun and fabulous tools and supplies in the first place!

What are some fun ideas for using paper scraps, leftover stickers and rub-ons, or old supplies?

Waste not, want not! In your stash of old supplies lurks unleashed creativity. Leftover stickers and rub-ons can spruce up a background, add oomph to home-dec projects, become that "little something special" on a child's school project and so much more. Schedule time each month to visit with your unused supplies, jotting down creative ideas. Let the supplies challenge you to be more creative with usage. If a year passes, and you don't use a supply, get rid of it.

"Knock, knock"
"Who's there?"
"Banana"
"Banana who?"

"Knock, knock"
"Who's there?"
"Banana"
"Banana who?"

"Knock, knock"
"Who's there?"
"Banana"
"Banana who?"

"Knock, knock"
"Who's there?"
"Orange"
"Orange who?"
"Orange you glad I didn't say banana?!"

No matter how many times I hear it. I never get tired of it. It's your favorite joke, maybe your only joke. You think it is hilarious, and that is what matters. Sometimes you forget how many times you've said "banana" and the joke just keeps going!

Michaela at 5

SUPPLIES:
Patterned paper (Autumn Leaves, K & Company, Making Memories, Provo Craft, Scenic Route Paper Co.); rub-ons (Déjà Views, Mustard Moon); brads (Making Memories) epoxy word (Junkitz); silk flowers; cardstock

Angelia

Customize a Background

Angelia savors her scrap heap of patterned paper because it allows her to create interesting page backgrounds. On this page, she mixed several patterns, adding a curving strip of black-and-white patterned paper for eye-popping interest. She used a mix of leftover rub-ons for an eclectic title.

102

Decorate a Frame

"Fun, funky and decorative." Those are Susan's words to describe this frame, which came together from a mishmash of leftover ribbon, rub-ons and epoxy stickers. Working with scraps was a great way for Susan to experiment with mixing styles without the fear of using up precious supplies.

SUPPLIES:
Frame (Bazzill); acrylic paint; chipboard accent (Heidi Swapp); rhinestones (Westrim); ribbon (American Crafts, May Arts, Strano); rub-ons (American Crafts, Making Memories); epoxy stickers (Junkitz)

Susan W.

Expert Advice!

How to organize paper scraps and leftover supplies:

* Organize leftover cardstock by color and patterned paper by color or theme. Scraps can be contained in stackable plastic drawers, hanging file folders or flat racks.

* Organize stickers, rub-ons and die cuts by style, color or theme.

Spice Up a Magnetic Board

Julie

"To do" lists have never been more inviting than the ones placed on this pretty magnetic board. Julie added some chic style to this mesh magnetic board with some leftover paper, ribbon, buttons and rub-on scraps. The colorful daisy magnets were created with the help of another scrap—old magnetic business cards. Julie put them in her daisy punch, covered them with paper punched from the same punch and then stuck them on the board, where they could add their own creative punch.

SUPPLIES:
Mesh magnetic board, metal accessories (Making Memories); patterned paper, ribbon, buttons (SEI); rub-ons (Junkitz); flower punch (EK Success); magnetic strips

What do I need to know about fabric before using it on my page? What are some creative ways to include it?

For some scrapbookers, fabric is the new patterned paper. It is available in just as many colors, styles and patterns, if not more, as patterned paper. It's durable and has a reach-out-and-touch-me texture that patterned paper, no matter how cool, can't replicate. When using fabric on your page, consider applying an iron-on stabilizer, which will stiffen it. To attach fabric to your page, we definitely recommend sewing, but it can also be secured with staples, brads and adhesive. Use large pieces or rip strips to tie in knots or use for borders.

MY SWEET, SWEET BABY GIRL

Aysha, when I look at this photo of you I feel so many emotions. I can't believe that you are the same little baby that I gave birth to over 10 years ago. you have grown and changed so much. I know we probably have many difficult times ahead of us as you enter your teenage years, but if you always remember how much I love you, we'll make it through together just fine.

March 2003

SUPPLIES:
Patterned papers (Sassafras Lass); cheesecloth (Wimpole Street); chipboard accents (Making Memories); date stamp (Scraptivity); die-cut letters, tag (QuicKutz); rhinestones, slide clip (Heidi Swapp); ribbon (American Crafts, May Arts); stamping ink; chalk; clear gloss medium; glitter glue; colored pencils

Trudy

Fabric Flowers

Many scrapbookers have been known to develop serious fabric addictions. There are just so many styles, patterns and textures to spark wild creativity. Trudy absolutely loves using fabric on scrapbook pages, and her favorite is cheesecloth. "It comes in a variety of colors and can be easily dyed to be the perfect shade," she says. "It has a wonderful, light airy feel to it." On this layout, she fashioned flowers from cheesecloth. She gathered the material and secured the center with flower brads.

Themed Accents

You'll have much better luck working with fabric to create embellishments if you stabilize it first with cardstock, Lisa says. Also, when sewing fabric to a page, be sure to hold it taut to prevent gaps and bubbles. For the pumpkin accent, Lisa cut a pattern from cardstock. She then cut fabric to fit the pattern. To adhere the fabric to the cardstock, she ran the cardstock pieces through an adhesive-application machine. Finally, she reassembled the accent and matted it with felt.

SUPPLIES:
Chipboard accents (Everlasting Keepsakes, Heidi Swapp); letter stickers (Scenice Route Paper Co.) buttons (Foofala); ribbon (Michaels); embroidery floss; fabric; cardstock

Lisa V.

Stamped Fabric Accents

Fabric can be an absolute pain in the butt to adhere to your scrapbook page, but it can be done. If you're not into sewing, we don't recommend using fabric to build an entire background. Unless you're working with self-adhesive sheets of fabric, gluing the fabric can be and look messy. Instead, opt for simple fabric accents. Vanessa cut fabric shapes with a die-cutter (for best results, apply stabilizer to fabric before cutting) and then stamped on them. She adhered them to the background with glue dots.

SUPPLIES:
Patterned paper, ribbon (American Crafts); silk flowers (Heidi Swapp); die-cut flowers (Sizzix); brads (Making Memories); letter stamps (Technique Tuesday); rub-ons (K & Company); stamping ink; cardstock; fonts (www.twopeasinabucket.com, www.scrapvillage.com)

Vanessa

I love using ribbon as frilly borders and tag toppers. Are there more fun ways to use it?

Are you kidding? There's a bazillion, gazillion ways to use ribbon! Ribbon can be used in much the same way as any other scrapbook supply. Take paper, for instance. You can run lengths of ribbon across a piece of cardstock to create a background or stretch it across a page to create a border, much like you would a strip of paper. Need to secure something to your page? Think ribbon! Out of accents? Tie a bunch of little bows or knots and attach with an adhesive dot.

SUPPLIES:
Patterned papers, rhinestones, flowers, photo corner (K & Company); chipboard accents (Heidi Swapp); rub-ons (Making Memories); ribbon (Michaels); decorative scissors; cardstock; font (Garamouche)

Pleat It

Pleated ribbon reminds us of school-girl skirts or frilly bedding trim. Here, Valerie used it to add texture to this page that details (gushes, perhaps) what she loves about her five-year-old daughter. To pleat the ribbon, she employed the help of her sewing machine (set to zigzag stitch). She folded the ribbon and ran it through the machine.

Weave It

If you're looking for a way to add flirty fun and a sense of movement, weave a strand of ribbon or rickrack through a larger strand. Here Angelia cut slits in the wide ribbon in which to thread a thinner strip of rickrack. She also add a toyish pink hinge to embellish the brown ribbon. Pink silk flowers and a vintage metal tag added further charm to this girly page.

SUPPLIES:
Patterned paper (Basic Grey, K & Co.); alphabet stickers (Basic Grey, Making Memories); 3D stickers, metal tag (K & Co.); ribbon (Offray); hinge (Daisy D's Paper Company); cardstock; rickrack

Angelia

Run It

The ribbon running rampant across this page is the perfect thematic design element. At first glance, we can see how it mimics the neon lights of the vintage theater marquee. But it also subconsciously relates to the film reels on a projector. Samantha cut snips of various ribbons and randomly placed them on the background. She then handwrote the journaling between the lines of ribbon for an imaginative touch.

SUPPLIES:
Ribbon (All My Memories, Making Memories, Offray); photo corners, charms (Nunn Designs); buckles (Making Memories); acrylic paint; hole punch; cardstock

Samantha

Expert Advice!

Use these supplies to secure ribbon to your page:

* Thread (stitch it with simple hand stitches—straight, zigzag or crisscross—or use the sewing machine)

* Heavy-duty double-sided tape

* Brads

* Adhesive dots

* Tape (run ribbon across the length of the layout and secure on the back of the page)

* Staples

Are cutting templates too "old school?" Please tell me they are still cool!

Cutting templates? Old school? No way! OK, so maybe they're not the hippest must-have scrapbooking product on the market, but they're totally useful and reliable. Without cutting templates, most of us would be pretty sloppy or simply avoid paper shapes all together. But, thankfully they exist to help us create whimsical backgrounds, nested shapes, photo mats and so much more.

Cuts in a Jiff

Peanut butter and jelly. Ketchup and mustard. Milk and cookies. Cutting templates and boldly patterned papers. All are a match made in heaven. "Some papers are so bold, they are best used in small amounts," Suzy says. She used a heart template to cut hearts in graduating sizes from some of her favorite patterned paper.

SUPPLIES:
Patterned papers (Imagination Project); textured papers (Fibermark); heart template; rub-ons (Déjà Views, Li'l Davis Designs); thread; pen

Suzy

PHOTO: TARA WHITNEY PHOTOGRAPHY

108

Perfect Nested Circles

Circles are such a versatile shape, and Vanessa loves her nested-circle cutting template for that very reason. Nested templates will allow you to cut circles in a variety of sizes. "Just get out the template and start playing," Vanessa pleads. For this layout, Vanessa used the template to create a border. The nested circle shapes mimic the time theme and help unify the cream paper with the polka-dot background.

SUPPLIES:
Patterned paper (My Mind's Eye); circle template (Provo Craft); clock stamp (Inkadinkado); chipboard accents (Heidi Swapp); stamping ink; clock hands; brads; cardstock; font (www.twopeasinabucket.com)

Vanessa

TIME well spent

Good quality time with your kids is a hard to thing to come by these days. Our lives seem so busy at times, but this day was different. Time seems to slow down when you're fishing. A little bait, the country air, and good conversation, doesn't even matter if the fish are biting. Savannah and Eric 8-12-05

Expert Advice!

Here are tips for getting great cuts with a craft knife:

* Always use a sharp blade.
* Hold the knife like a pencil.
* Orient your work toward you so the act of cutting occurs naturally.
* Try to make long, single cuts.

Totally Versatile

Cutting systems may seem a bit outdated, Shannon says, but that doesn't mean you can't put a fresh spin on them. Shannon used a diamond cutter to trim pink and black shapes from cardstock which she paired with rhinestone brads to create a regal, crownlike accent perched across the top of her page. "These systems are completely worth the money," Shannon says. "They make it very easy to mat shapes."

SUPPLIES:
Patterned papers (Junkitz); diamond cutter (Provo Craft); rhinestone brads; rhinestone buckle; chipboard glitter tile (Me & My Big Ideas); ribbon (American Crafts); rub-ons; cardstock

Have you ever seen butterfly bling? Well last year, our very own Miss Caroline celebrated Halloween as the flashiest butterfly i've ever seen. We're talking metal chains, sequins and glittery wings. She looked beautiful! 2005

BLING

Shannon

I'm lost when it comes to using found objects. Please show me the way.

Identifying the perfect found objects to use on your pages is definitely a journey of discovery. Just like the name states, the objects can be found almost anywhere, and the best found objects are often small, flat and lightweight. Popular destinations include any of the following stores: office supply, craft, hardware, fabric, toy, grocery, flea markets, antique. But let's not forget the veritable treasure chests that are our junk drawers, hope chests, jewelry boxes, kids' rooms, garage sales…hey, why not look under the couch cushions, too?

Kelly

SUPPLIES:
Patterned papers (Basic Grey); chipboard accents (Grafix, Heidi Swapp); transparent accent (Heidi Swapp); pens; paper fastener; spiral clips; notebook paper; compass; staples; cardstock

Office Accents

When adding found objects to this page, Kelly looked no further than her desk drawer. She loves the big, silver paper fasteners, which remind her of brads, she says. Also, she created chipboardlike accents by punching shapes from cardboard that she tore off the back of a legal pad. The notebook paper completes the look.

Sewing Supplies

When Diana looks for found objects to use on her page, she first asks herself, "What will work, thematically?" On this page, several sewing supplies helped give it a vintage look, but the playing card carries the most symbolism. "The number, the hearts and the color red made it the perfect choice for my title block," she says.

SUPPLIES:
Patterned paper, border stickers, bookplate, rub-ons, chipboard accent (Making Memories); corner punch (EK Success); playing card; snap; rickrack; staples; thread

Diana H.

Nature Supplies

Your front yard can hold a bounty of found objects, although extra special care needs to be taken when using them. Amber used a large twig on this page, which features her friend and her friend's son in a tender moment. Amber enhanced the twig with fake berries and leaves, giving the page a real fall feel. When creating such accents, be sure the page, once placed in an album, has ample room and that the accent will not harm photos on other pages.

SUPPLIES:
Patterned paper (Daisy D's); cardstock buttons (Autumn Leaves); tag (7 Gypsies); chipboard letters (Heidi Swapp); acrylic paint; thread; hemp cord; fabric; artificial berries and leaves; twig

Amber

PHOTO: VICKI BOUTIN

I have brads and eyelets coming out of my ears. Give me some unconventional ways to use them.

If you started scrapbooking in the late '90s/early millennium, surely you remember the splash that brads and eyelets caused in scrapbooking. They were everywhere. Every company made them in every color. Special tools were invented. Crops started to sound as if scrapbookers were banging out car dents instead of quietly adhering photos to cardstock. And, you couldn't buy just one or two, you bought them by the hundreds. Not a big deal, really, because these little guys have a million uses.

SUPPLIES:
Patterned paper (Crafter's Workshop, Sassafras Lass); brads (Junkitz, Queen & Co.); chipboard letter (Making Memories); acrylic paint; stamping ink; eyelets; letter stamps (PSX Design); colored pencils; cardstock

Nic

PHOTO: SHARYN DE JONGE

Accent an Accent

Swirls and doodles are very en vogue in scrapbook page design. Rather than create them by hand, why not use brads and eyelets to fashion the design? Originally, Nic thought she might enhance these flower accents with doodles, which would match their hand-drawn appearance. Upon further creative thinking, she started experimenting with brads and eyelets. She attached the brads and eyelets so they would appear to radiate from the flower petals. This technique gives the layout a pop that no doodle could ever achieve.

Embellish a Title

Holy cow! Kelly used forty brads on this layout! To mimic the look of the gingerbread house her sons were creating, Kelly sprinkled her title and page accents with brightly colored brads. "I think the brads made my title look like candy," Kelly says. Yum!

When I saw this Gingerbread House kit, I had to have it. I'll admit, it was more for me than for you, but we had such fun decorating it together. I did all the icing work and the three of you put on the candy & trimmings. (What you didn't eat first, that is - just look at Carson's mouth!) When we were finished, it looked good enough to eat. And well, you tried that, too!

december 17th

2005

before

after

Kelly

SUPPLIES:
Patterned paper (Designs by Reminisce, KI Memories); transparent letters, chipboard accents (Heidi Swapp); letter stickers (Bo-Bunny Press); brads (Queen & Co.); cardstock; pens; stamping ink; font (Century Gothic)

"Eyelets are so versatile! They can be used to attach things, thread things through or just hang out on their own. And what could be more fun to add to a layout than something that you have to use a hammer to install?" **Sheila**

Bind a Book and String a Fiber

Those super-duper big eyelets? They are great for binding mini albums, as Samantha has shown us here. They are strong and wide enough to accommodate more than a few pages. Those eyelets that come in packs of coordinating colors? Those are fantastic border accents. Again, Samantha used them to border the edges of the album and then she laced a delicate ribbon through them. Brads? Well, Samantha made them look pretty snazzy as a modern geometric design element.

SUPPLIES:
Patterned paper, stickers (Creative Imaginations); grommets, eyelets (Prym Dritz); kraft paper (Provo Craft); ribbon (Offray); chipboard, binder rings, brads (Making Memories); stamping ink

Samantha

Stickers and die cuts are about as exciting as dirty laundry, but I have SO many. Make them exciting for me again!

In today's scrapbooking climate, where the market is inundated with snazzy products that have dimension, sparkle or superfly funk, simple paper accents seem a little lackluster. Yet let's not forget why we were drawn to stickers and die cuts in the first place: 1. They are easy to work with. 2. They come in every theme, color and style imaginable. 3. They are made of paper, and therefore we can manipulate them in all sorts of ways. 4. They are super safe to use in our scrapbooks. 5. They were our first love, so they'll always have a special place in our hearts.

my one true love

We were so excited when Bob and Tiffany got engaged. They are so in love- and she's perfect for him! 2005

Jessie

SUPPLIES:
Patterned paper (Fancy Pants Designs); stickers (EK Success); stamps (Technique Tuesday); acrylic paint; buttons; thread; stamping ink; pen; cardstock

Use Them as Masks

"For Halloween?!" you ask. Sure, why not...now you're thinking creatively and like a pro! Actually, we meant masks in the sense that the stickers would be used to create a resist effect by covering part of an image or background that is to be painted. Jessie used flower stickers to mask parts of an enlarged photo and patterned paper that she painted white. To relieve the sticker of some of its tackiness, she first stuck it to her jeans a few times. Then she applied the stickers to her page, painted away and, once the paint dried, removed them to leave a negative image. Cool!

Add Snazz with Glitter and Brads

Glitter just makes everything better. Layout too drab? Add some glitter. Need more of a feminine touch? Glitter. Feel as if you could give your kids up for adoption? Well, maybe glitter plus a little "me" time will remedy those feelings. Here, Susan glitzed up some old snowflake die cuts with glittery embossing powder. She then attached them to her page with colorful brads and lifted the snowflake edges just a bit for some dimension.

SUPPLIES:
Patterned paper (Scenic Route Paper Co.); snowflake die (QuicKutz); cardstock; ribbon, stickers, rub-ons (American Crafts); brads (Queen & Co.); glitter embossing powder; thread

Susan W.

Hip 'em Up With Trendy Stuff

If your sticker and die-cut collection bores you to tears, just think of the products that really excite you. Then, figure out a way to use what you love to infuse what you used to love with new life. For this mini album, Amber decided to combine some old stickers and die cuts with chipboard and distressing techniques. On the cover of the album, the entire bottom half is, yep, stickers. Some she mounted onto chipboard and then added for a dimensional effect. The funky flower? She used an old die cut to trace the flower onto her current favorite patterned paper. She cut it out and then distressed the petals and added faux stitching details with pen.

SUPPLIES:
Patterned paper, stickers (K & Company); die cuts (K & Company, My Mind's Eye); buttons (Autumn Leaves); thread; hemp; chipboard; ribbon; binder rings; font (www.twopeasinabucket.com)

Amber

I have more sets of alphabet stamps than shoes (seriously). Remind me of some fun ways to use my ABC arsenal.

Collectively, we can't decide if having more sets of alphabet stamps than shoes is a good thing or bad thing. No matter, both shoes and alphabet stamps hold a special place in our hearts. First of all, stamps of any kind are economical. If you buy stamps that you truly love and will use again and again, they are a sound purchase. Second, the eclectic look is in, so the best way to use all these stamps is to mix up the styles on your layouts. Go bold and be sassy!

Jennifer B.

SUPPLIES:
Patterned paper (Doodlebug Design, FontWerks); letter stamps (Li'l Davis Designs, Making Memories); letter stamps (PSX Design); acrylic paint; circle punch; rhinestone brads (SEI); photo turns (Junkitz); lollipop stick

Stamp a Design Element

What's ONE good thing about this layout? If we had to pick just ONE thing (hint, hint), it would be Jennifer's super attention to ONE detail! For this layout, Jennifer wanted to play up the first birthday theme. She used mini alphabet stamps to do that by stamping the word "one" repeatedly on the layout. In the title, she accented the large word "one" by stamping the letters of the word inside the bigger corresponding letters with the smaller stamps. Then, she sprinkled her journaling with the stamped word.

Create Patterned Paper

Tired of titles? Just done with journaling blocks? Fine, dust off the old ABC stamps to create some custom background paper. For this layout, Kelly stamped large letters onto brightly colored cardstock for an ABC background that was as easy as 1, 2, 3. She then cut the letters out and adhered them in alphabetical order onto black background paper.

SUPPLIES:
Letter stickers (American Crafts); letter stamps (Technique Tuesday); cardstock; stamping ink; pen

Kelly

Stamp a Frame

With time and patience, you too can create a stamped descriptive-word border in which to frame an adorable focal photo. Valerie will not lie about the fact that this technique is a little time consuming, but she swears, "It's worth it!" Gather a few sets of stamps and stamp the words, alternating the stamp styles for each letter. For extra pop, add a similar border under a series of photos.

SUPPLIES:
Patterned papers (Chatterbox); letter stickers (Basic Grey); clear epoxy circle stickers (K & Co.); letter stamps (EK Success, Hero Arts, K & Company, PSX Design); stamping ink; cardstock; font (Prissy Frat Boy)

Valerie S.

I think I'm severely underestimating the power of my pens and markers. How can I use this staple supply more creatively?

It's easy to take something as everyday as a pen for granted. We use them so much for the function of written communication that it's hard for some to look at them as a creative tool. Not to mention that most of us have hang-ups about our penmanship or the fact that by age thirty, we still can't draw a decent stick figure. Even if you feel you don't possess pen prowess, there is something creative, easy and doable you can do with your pens and markers.

Danielle

PHOTO: ALLISON WESTOVER

SUPPLIES:
Rhinestones (Westrim);
mini file folder (Paper Loft);
pens; foam; embroidery floss;
staples; cardstock

Oodles of Background Doodles

Danielle's layered background is doodliscious. She wanted to create the look of waves. She started by choosing a serene mix of blue and green cardstock. She then drew freehand doodle waves with green, blue and white pens, cut them out and adhered them to the background. After adding delicate stitched swirl details, she adhered the title, which she cut from self-adhesive foam.

Doodle Dingbats

Admittedly, Jenn says she is not a doodler (gasp!). But, she likes the look doodles can give a layout—that look of footloose-and-fancy-free, mind-wandering glee. So, like any determined scrapbooker, she found a way to neatly imitate the look of a doodle. She found a dingbat font that she liked and printed some characters onto white paper. With the help of her trusty lightbox, she then transferred the doodles onto patterned paper. She cut out the accents and sprinkled them on the page.

SUPPLIES:
Patterned paper (Chatterbox, SEI); photo corner (Heidi Swapp); stamping ink; pen; cardstock

Jenn B.

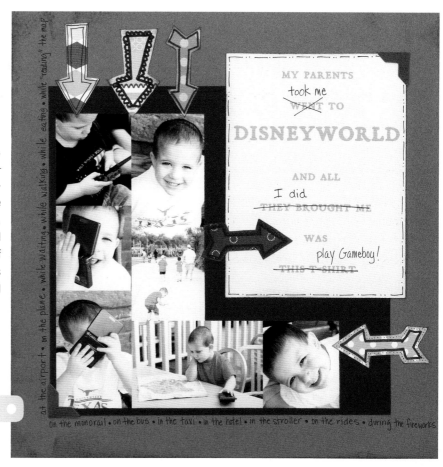

Doodle Dandy Accents

Always the artist, Suzy used her pens to draw this precious ballet shoe image. For the delicate shading, she used brush markers in a variety of tips. To smooth the shading, she used a blending pen. If you are not a strong illustrator, try stamping an image on your page and coloring it in with pens and markers.

SUPPLIES:
Patterned paper (My Mind's Eye); buttons (Making Memories); rhinestones (Darice, Me & My Big Ideas); pens; embroidery floss; cardstock

Suzy

PHOTO: TARA WHITNEY PHOTOGRAPHY

I own a basic shadow-stamp set. Remind me, why did I buy these simple stamp shapes?

Shadow stamps: you bought them because they are practical and versatile, and they were probably on sale! Actually, they are a really handy tool for a scrapbooker to own. Shadow stamps create solid geometric shapes, such as circles and blocks. You can use them to create a background for another stamp (e.g., stamp a square shadow stamp and, once the image dries, stamp a flower image on top), custom page backgrounds, backgrounds for titles and more.

Valerie S.

SUPPLIES:
Patterned paper (source unknown); chipboard accents (Pressed Petals); shadow stamps (Hero Arts); stamping ink; sticker, charm (K & Company); ribbon, rub-on letter (source unknown); cardstock

Awesome Accents

What a tangled web Valerie weaves, deceptively using a shadow stamp for not a background, but a prominent accent full of saturated color! As she created this page about her son's fascination with Spider-Man, she knew she wanted some kind of design element that would echo the irregular block shapes of Spider-Man's web. She pulled out her shadow stamps to create layered block accents in the trademark red and blue of the superhero's uniform.

STAMPING INK TUTORIAL
The different types of stamping inks defined.

Dye ink | This water-based ink results in delicate color. It is quick-drying, but not lightfast or fade resistant.

Chalk ink | Also a water-based ink, when dry, this ink has the appearance of chalk. The resulting colors are more saturated than dye inks, but also like dye inks, chalk inks are not lightfast or fade resistant.

Watermark ink | This water-based ink is available clear or slightly tinted. It produces a tone-on-tone effect, which makes it great for creating backgrounds on cardstock.

Pigment ink | This archival-quality ink is the best bet for your scrapbooks. It is lightfast and fade resistant but is slow-drying. It is a natural choice for heat embossing.

Solvent ink | When you wish to stamp on a non-porous surface, such as plastic or metal, reach for the solvent ink. Solvent ink should not be used on photos because it is not of archival quality.

Photo Frames

With a little ingenuity, Suzy has caused shadow stamps to transcend from basic background usage to full-on, look-at-me attention getters. To drive home the fact that she and her son look amazingly alike, she created mini frames to highlight their faces in the support photos. She stamped basic blocks with her shadow stamp and trimmed them into mini frames.

SUPPLIES:
Patterned paper, letter stickers (Basic Grey); shadow stamp (Hero Arts); buttons (Making Memories); embroidery floss; stamping ink; pens; cardstock

Suzy

PHOTO: TARA WHITNEY PHOTOGRAPHY

I own a punch set of basic shapes.
Give me fresh punch-art accent ideas.

Clear your calendar because we're going to show you punch art so exquisite and detailed that you're going to spend hours re-creating it. Just kidding! There was a time when really involved punch-art designs were the rage, but most of today's scrapbookers prefer the more practical side of punching. A punch set of basic shapes has a bevy of uses. You can create backgrounds, themed or geometric accents, photo corners, tags, bouncing borders, labels, captions, titles and journaling block accents, photo mats…we could go on and on.

Angelia

SUPPLIES:
Patterned papers, chipboard letters, die-cut flowers (K & Company); letter stickers (Basic Grey); brads (Making Memories); circle punch; cardstock

Definitive Design Element

When considering punch art, Angelia recommends, "Think beyond small punch art, and you can create a graphic background that will never go out of style." Angelia's technique is easy, and it's a great way to use up paper scraps. Take a basic circle punch, grab some patterned paper and start punching. Quick tip: Run the patterned paper through an adhesive-application machine before you punch for easy placement. Angelia placed the circles on the background so they would overlap the photo, which gives the page depth and draws the eye to the image of her beautiful daughter.

Funky Frame

This page contains a funky bunch of punched accents. The most obvious act as a one-sided photo frame that helps draw the eye to the photo. Jessica simply used two sizes of square punches to create them. The other accents are a bit more nonchalant. The date tab at the top right was created with a couple of circle punches. Finally, the cute parentheses that wrap around the word "sorta" in the title are the result of a circle punch. Jessica punched a circle and then used the same punch to punch out two crescents from the same circle.

SUPPLIES:
Patterned paper (KI Memories, My Mind's Eye); chipboard letters (KI Memories); square and circle punches; font (Century Gothic, Impact); cardstock

Jessica

Big, Bad Border

Next time you are stumped for a layout idea, pick up a piece of your favorite patterned paper. Now, look at the design to see if it can be mimicked with a simple punch-art creation. That is exactly what Jodi did for this page. She loves the patterned paper shown in the strip that stretches across the title. For this page, the bold pattern was best used in a small amount, but she needed a way to incorporate it into her design cohesively. Since the pattern consisted of basic geometric shapes, she broke out her punch set to create a cool border that echoes the design. She also punched small circles to create a dotted design element that connects the portrait to the title.

SUPPLIES:
Patterned paper (We R Memory Keepers); letter accents (Heidi Swapp); flowers (Prima); circle punches, square punches; rub-ons (Lasing Impressions); brads (Bazzill); cardstock

Jodi H.

sources

The following companies manufacture products featured in this book. Please check your local retailers to find these materials, or go to a company's Web site for the latest product. In addition, we have made every attempt to properly credit the items mentioned in this book. We apologize to any company that we have listed incorrectly, and we would appreciate hearing from you.

3 BUGS IN A RUG
(801) 804-6657
www.3bugsinarug.com

7 GYPSIES
(877) 749-7797
www.sevengypsies.com

ADOBE SYSTEMS
INCORPORATED
(866) 766-2256
www.adobe.com

ALL MY MEMORIES
(888) 553-1998
www.allmymemories.com

ALL NIGHT MEDIA
(see Plaid Enterprises)

AMERICAN CRAFTS
(801) 226-0747
www.americancrafts.com

ANNA GRIFFIN, INC.
(888) 817-8170
www.annagriffin.com

AROUND THE BLOCK
(801) 593-1946
www.aroundtheblock
products.com

AUTUMN LEAVES
(800) 588-6707
www.autumnleaves.com

AVERY DENNISON
CORPORATION
(800) GO-AVERY
www.avery.com

BASIC GREY™
(801) 451-6006
www.basicgrey.com

BAZZILL BASICS PAPER
(480) 558-8557
www.bazzillbasics.com

BERWICK OFFRAY™, LLC
(800) 344-5533
www.offray.com

BLUE MOON BEADS
(800) 377-6715
www.bluemoonbeads.com

BO-BUNNY PRESS
(801) 771-4010
www.bobunny.com

BOUTIQUE TRIMS, INC.
(248) 437-2017
www.boutiquetrims.com

BOXER SCRAPBOOK
PRODUCTIONS
(503) 625-0455
www.boxerscrapbooks.com

CARL MFG. USA, INC.
(800) 257-4771
www.Carl-Products.com

CAROLEE'S CREATIONS®
(435) 563-1100
www.ccpaper.com

CHATTERBOX, INC.
(208) 939-9133
www.chatterboxinc.com

CHERRY ARTE
(212) 465-3495
www.cherryarte.com

CRAFTER'S WORKSHOP, THE
(877) CRAFTER
www.thecraftersworkshop.com

CRATE PAPER
www.cratepaper.com

CREATIVE IMAGINATIONS
(800) 942-6487
www.cigift.com

CREATIVE IMPRESSIONS
RUBBER STAMPS, INC.
(719) 596-4860
www.creativeimpressions.com

CREATIVE MEMORIES®
(800) 468-9335
www.creativememories.com

DAISY D'S PAPER
COMPANY
(888) 601-8955
www.daisydspaper.com

DARICE, INC.
(800_ 321-1494
www.darice.com

DÈJÁ VIEWS
(800) 243-8419
www.dejaviews.com

DELUXE DESIGNS
(480) 497-9005
www.deluxedesigns.com

DESIGN ORIGINALS
(800) 877-0067
www.d-originals.com

DESIGNS BY REMINISCE
(319) 358-9777
www.designsbyreminisce.com

DIE CUTS WITH A VIEW
(801) 224-6766
www.diecutswithaview.com

DMC CORP.
(973) 589-0606
www.dmc.com

DOODLEBUG DESIGN™ INC.
(801) 966-9952
www.doodlebug.ws

DOVER PUBLICATIONS, INC.
(800) 223-3130
www.doverpublications.com

EGGERY PLACE, THE
www.theeggeryplace.com

EK SUCCESS™, LTD.
(800) 524-1349
www.eksuccess.com

EVERLASTING
KEEPSAKES™
(816) 896-7037
www.everlastinkeepsakes.com

FAMILY TREASURES®
(949) 290-0872
www.familytreasures.com

FANCY PANTS DESIGNS, LLC
(801) 779-3212
www.fancypantsdesigns.com

FIBERMARK
(802) 257-0365
http://scrapbook.fibermark.com

FISKARS®, INC.
(800) 950-0203
www.fiskars.com

FONTWERKS
(604) 942-3105
www.fontwerks.com

FOOFALA
(402) 330-3208
www.foofala.com

FRANCES MEYER, INC.®
(413) 584-5446
www.francesmeyer.com

GRAFIX®
(800) 447-2349
www.grafix.com

HEIDI SWAPP/
ADVANTUS
CORPORATION
(904) 482-0092
www.heidiswapp.com

HERO ARTS® RUBBER
STAMPS, INC.
(800) 822-4376
www.heroarts.com

IMAGINATION PROJECT, INC.
(513) 860-2711
www.imaginationproject.com

INKADINKADO® RUBBER
STAMPS
(800) 888-4652
www.inkadinkado.com

JENNIFER COLLECTION, THE
(518) 272-4572
www.paperdiva.com

JEWELCRAFT, LLC
(201) 223-0804
www.jewelcraft.biz

JO-ANN STORES
(888) 739-4120
www.joann.com

JUNKITZ™
(732) 792-1108
www.junkitz.com

JUSTRITE® STAMPERS/
MILLENIUM MARKING
COMPANY
(847) 806-1750
www.justritestampers.com

K & COMPANY
(888) 244-2083
www.kandcompany.com

KAREN FOSTER DESIGN
(801) 451-9779
www.karenfosterdesign.com

KI MEMORIES
(972) 243-5595
www.kimemories.com

KRYLON®
(216) 566-200
www.krylon.com

LASTING IMPRESSIONS
FOR PAPER, INC.
(801) 298-1979
www.lastingimpressions.com

LAZAR STUDIOWERX, INC.
(866) 478-9379
www.lazarstudiowerx.com

LEAVE MEMORIES
www.leavememories.com

LI'L DAVIS DESIGNS
(949) 838-0344
www.lildavisdesigns.com

LIQUITEX® ARTIST
MATERIALS
(888) 4-ACRYLIC
www.liquitex.com

MAGIC SCRAPS™
(972) 238-1838
www.magicscraps.com

MAKING MEMORIES
(800) 286-5263
www.makingmemories.com

MAY ARTS
(800) 442-3950
www.mayarts.com

MAYA ROAD, LLC
(214) 488-3279
www.mayaroad.com

ME & MY BIG IDEAS®
(949) 883-2065
www.meandmybigideas.com

MEMORIES
COMPLETE™, LLC
(866) 966-6365
www.memoriescomplete.com

MICHAELS®
ARTS & CRAFTS
(800) 642-4235
www.michaels.com

MULBERRY INVITATIONS
(714) 575-1171
www.mulberryinvitations.com

MUSTARD MOON™
(408) 299-8542
www.mustardmoon.com

MY MIND'S EYE™, INC.
(800) 665-5116
www.frame-ups.com

MY FONTS
www.myfonts.com

NRN DESIGNS
(800) 421-6958
www.nrndesigns.com

NUNN DESIGN
(360) 379-3557
www.nunndesign.com

OFFRAY – see Berwick Offray, LLC

OLD NAVY
(800) 653-6289
www.oldnavy.com

P22 TYPE FOUNDRY
(800) 722-5080
www.P22.com

PAPER HOUSE
PRODUCTIONS®
(800) 255-7316
www.paperhouseproductions.com

PAPER LOFT
(866) 254-1961
www.paperloft.com

PAPER STUDIO
(480) 557-5700
www.paperstudio.com

PEBBLES INC.
(801) 224-1857
www.pebblesinc.com

PIXIE PRESS
www.hsn.com

PLAID ENTERPRISES, INC.
(800) 842-4197
www.plaidonline.com

PRESSED PETALS
(800) 748-4656
www.pressedpetals.com

PRIMA MARKETING, INC.
(909) 627-5532
www.mulberrypaperflowers.com

PRISM™ PAPERS
(866) 902-1002
www.prismpapers.com

PROVO CRAFT®
(888) 577-3545
www.provocraft.com

PRYM-DRITZ CORPORATION
www.dritz.com

PSX DESIGN™
(800) 782-6748
www.psxdesign.com

PUNCH BUNCH, THE
(254) 791-4209
www.thepunchbunch.com

QUEEN & CO.
(858) 485-5132
www.queenandcompany.com

QUICKUTZ, INC.
(801) 765-1144
www.quickutz.com

RUSTY PICKLE
(801) 746-1045
www.rustypickle.com

SANDYLION STICKER DE-
SIGNS
(800) 387-4215
www.sandylion.com

SASSAFRAS LASS
(801) 269-1331
www.sassafraslass.com

SCENIC ROUTE PAPER CO.
(801) 785-0761
www.scenicroutepaper.com

SCRAP SUPPLY
(615) 777-3953
www.scrapsupply.com

SCRAPTIVITY™
SCRAPBOOKING, INC.
(800) 393-2151
www.scraptivity.com

SCRAP VILLAGE
www.scrapvillage.com

SCRAPWORKS, LLC
(801) 363-1010
www.scrapworks.com

SEI, INC.
(800) 333-3279
www.shopsei.com

SIZZIX®
(866) 742-4447
www.sizzix.com

STAMPENDOUS!®
(800) 869-0474
www.stampendous.com

STRANO DESIGNS
(508) 454-4615
www.stranodesigns.com

TARGET
www.target.com

TECHNIQUE TUESDAY, LLC
(503) 644-4073
www.techniquetuesday.com

THERM O WEB, INC.
(800) 323-0799
www.thermoweb.com

TRIM DESIGNS
(770) 518-9339
www.trimdesigns.com

TWO PEAS IN A BUCKET
(888) 896-7327
www.twopeasinabucket.com

URBAN ARTS AND CRAFTS
(816) 234-1004
www.urbanartsandcrafts.com

WAL-MART STORES, INC.
(800) WALMART
www.walmart.com

WE R MEMORY KEEPERS,
INC.
(801) 539-5000
www.weronthenet.com

WESTRIM® CRAFTS
(800) 727-2727
www.westrimcrafts.com

WIMPOLE STREET
CREATIONS
(801) 298-0504
www.wimpolestreet.com

WRIGHTS® RIBBON
ACCENTS
(877) 597-4448
www.wrights.com

XYRON
(800) 793-3523
www.xyron.com

ZETTIOLOGY RUBBER
STAMPS
www.teeshamoore.com

index

Check out these other books by Memory Makers Masters

THE SCRAPBOOKER'S ESSENTIAL GUIDE TO COLOR

Learn from the 2005 Memory Makers Masters how to create attractive color schemes that include monochromatic, analogous, complementary, split complementary, diad and triad combinations. Includes a bonus color wheel.

Z0020 $24.99

ISBN-10: 1-892127-80-6

ISBN-13: 978-1-892127-80-8

MASTERING SCRAPBOOK STYLES

Learn how to master essential elements of scrapbooking such as journaling, texture, design, color, typography and more in all-new ways from the 2004 Memory Makers Masters.

33361 $22.99

ISBN-10: 1-892124-55-5

ISBN-13: 978-1-892127-55-6

SCRAPBOOK EMBELLISHMENTS

The 2003 Memory Makers Masters offer inspiration and direction for enhancing scrapbook pages with embellishments. Discover 150+ sample pages using textiles, organics, metallics, papercrafts, baubles and more.

32998 $22.99

ISBN-10: 1-892127-31-8

ISBN-13: 978-1-892127-31-0